be my "flying buddy"
Don't ever give [...]
you any time. Wh[...]
bonds of Earth number, you're only
limited by your imagination!

— Th[...]

Her Mentor Was An Albatross

Her Mentor Was An Albatross

The Autobiography of Pioneer Pilot Harriet Quimby

Henry M. Holden

Mt. Freedom, N. J.

Copyright © 1993 Black Hawk Publishing Company

Printed in the United States of America. All rights reserved. No part of this book may be reproduced transmitted in any form or by any means, electronic or mechanical, including photocopying, recording by any information storage or retrieval system - except by a reviewer who may quote brief passeges in review to be printed in a newspaper or magazine, without permission in writing from the publisher. I information contact Black Hawk Publishing Company, P.O. Box 24, Mt. Freedom, N.J. 07970-0024.

First Edition - First Printing May 1993.

Cataloging in Publication

Holden, Henry M.
   Her mentor was an albatross : the autobiography of pioneer pilot Harriet Quim
/ by Henry M. Holden
   p.cm.
   includes bibliographical references and index.

ISBN 1-879630-05-2

1. Quimby, Harriet, 1875-1912--Biography. 2. Air Pilots--Women--Biography.
Women--United States--Biography. 4. Biography--Women--United States. I. Tit

TL540.Q9H6 1991   629.13092

Printed on recycled paper

Table of Contents

Introduction

Until now there have been few people who know about Harriet Quimby, and her tragically short life. "It is as if she never existed," wrote one Chicago columnist in 1977.

Who is Harriet Quimby and what did she do? There is little mention of Harriet Quimby in history books, and those references are sketchy and inconclusive. Quimby was a successful journalist, the first American woman to earn her pilot's license, the first to fly a monoplane, the first woman in the world to make a night flight, and to fly the English Channel. She earned acclaim from some people and scorn from others. She broke social norms and did things women in the early 1900s were not supposed to do. She was a fearless, independent young woman who had self-confidence, beauty, ambition, personality and brains.

Harriet Quimby did not marry, drove an automobile, used a camera, a typewriter and flew an airplane. Any of these individually would have been a problem for Victorian men, but all of these accomplishments rolled into one woman were impossible for most men to deal with. Quimby asserted her rights and encouraged other women to do the same. Any actions of an independent woman like Quimby whether or not associated with the growing Suffrage Movement were looked upon as "giving too much freedom to women." Men raised the question, "Where will it end?" Well we know it never "ended" and the fight for equality continues today. In an ironic twist, Quimby suffered the rejection of the early feminists and was ignored by the suffrage movement.

Timing worked against Harriet Quimby. The loss of the ocean liner *Titanic* and 1,500 lives was an unprecedented catastrophe in April 1912. Her historic flight across the English Channel just a day before the *Titanic's* loss was buried under disaster headlines in newspapers around the world. In fact, the New York *Times* on April 16th, and 17th had every inch of their first eight pages devoted to coverage of the tragedy, and not a word about Harriet Quimby's great victory.

In spite of strong opposition, Quimby opened the door for women in aviation, and this was hard for the Victorian-bred male to accept. She and other women were not welcomed by the male fliers. Harriet represented an intrusion into what they regarded as an occupation belonging exclusively to man. Most male pilots resented her. Some were outspoken in their protests and said frankly it was not a woman's business. Others put it on a sentimental basis. It was dangerous, they said, and women should not be allowed to risk their lives in airplanes. No matter how it was put, it was self-serving for the men and destructive for the women.

Her untimely death less than a year after she had earned her pilot's license was the "escape valve" American society needed. If writers would not immortalize her, she would fade from the spotlight, and become nothing more than a footnote in history. Unfortunately that is exactly what happened until now. In the 80 years that have elapsed since her death, there has never been more than a brief article or reference to her in any print media in America. When Amelia Earhart came into the aviation spotlight, she talked about Quimby's accomplishments but the world was enthralled by Earhart and gave little notice to Quimby. In 1991, America finally came to grips with Harriet Quimby when the Post Office issued a stamp in her honor. That and the brief mention in the Congressional Record have been the only long overdue fame for this pioneer aviator.

Acknowledgements

Writing a book is never a one-person undertaking. Many people over a period of several years contribute to the end result. Often they do not realize just how helpful they have been and they may have even forgotten that we ever had a conversation or corresponded. From that perspective and the factor of several years passing it difficult to adequately acknowledge and thank all the people who have made this book possible. I will try and if I have omitted anyone it is unintentional.

There are several people who generously volunteered a significant portion of their time to help make this book an accurate and valuable reference. Jenny Beatty patiently edited the manuscript and made many constructive comments that improved the quality of the text.

Alice F. Hughes, of the Branch District Library, in Coldwater, Michigan, shared with me her years of "living " with the files of Harriet Quimby. She also shared copies of William and Ursula Quimby's marriage license, Harriet Quimby's death certificate and other documents that provided threads that helped weave the final story of Harriet Quimby.

In addition, Margaret Price of the Arroyo Grande (California) Public Library, and Virginia Crook, Head Librarian of the San Luis Obispo (California), Public Library, were also instrumental in providing information that helped me tie together fragraments of Harriet's life and see a bigger picture.

My thanks also to Pam McFadden who read early versions of the manuscript and made many suggestions to improve on this story. A special note of thanks to Mario Nicaretta, whose assistance in reproducing many of the old *Leslie's Illustrated Weekly* photos was invaluable, and Tony Carfora who spent hours struggling with me to develop a suitable cover design.

And, as so often in the past, Melissa Keiser, of the Smithsonian Institution Air & Space Research Library was generous with her time and helpful in uncovering some of the mystery of Harriet's life.

And of course I owe a special acknowledgement to Nancy, who supported and understood my need to write this history. To everyone, my thanks and best wishes.

About the Author:

Henry M. Holden has published more than 250 magazine and newspaper articles on travel, general interest, photography and aviation that have appeared in a New Jersey newspaper syndicate, the New York *Times* syndication and the *Miami Herald*. His work has appeared in various national magazines including, *US Air*, *Skylite* (in-flight magazine of Butler Aviation), *Peterson's Photographic*, *Tallahassee Magazine*, *Florida Living* and various aviation magazines including the prestigious American Aviation Historical Society's *Journal*, and *Aviation Heritage*. Henry Holden is also an award-winning photographer whose photographs often appear with his work. He lectures frequently on aviation and business topics. He is currrently working on his next book, *Straight Up - The Whirly-Girls International Women Helicopter Pilots.*

Professional Affiliations
The Aviation/Space Writers Association
The Aviation Hall of Fame of New Jersey
The International Women's Writing Guild

Other books by the author:

* *The Douglas DC-3*
* *The Boeing 247 - The World's First Modern Commercial Airplane.*
* *The Fabulous Ford Tri-Motors*
* *Ladybirds - The Untold Story of Women Pilots in America* (with Capt. Lori Griffith)
* *Ladybirds II - The Continuing Story of American Women in Aviation* (& Capt. Lori Griffith)

Author's Note:

Traditional biographies often place the writer looking over the shoulder of the person about whom they are writing, whose words they are interpreting. The autobiography, on the other hand, places the reader directly in the mind of the chief protagonist, seeing the world through that person's eyes. The reader lives events as they occurred, experiences the thrills, and sorrows, as the subject experienced them. The combination of autobiography and "other voices" permits the biographer to widen the point of view, and to get a better perspective on the subject playing the lead. It allows the reader to see the person as the world saw her.

This is the story of an authentic American-born heroine who continued up to the day she took her last breath to fight for women's rights on the ground and in the air. It is built on many of the autobiographical articles written in the first person, that Harriet left behind. It is also complimented by the writings of others, each of whom saw Harriet Quimby through their own eyes. These "other voices" offer unique perspectives on the person of Harriet Quimby.

Harriet was loved by some and no doubt feared by others for what she represented, a liberated women who stood up for her rights. No one who encountered her was indifferent about her. To begin at the beginning it is sometimes necessary to start during the journey.

Chapter One

The Beginning

"The airplane should open a fruitful occupation for women. I see no reason they cannot realize handsome incomes by carrying passengers between adjacent towns, from parcel delivery, taking photographs or conducting schools of flying." - Harriet Quimby, 1911

Not in her wildest dreams could Harriet Quimby have imagined jets flying people from Los Angeles to New York in five hours. Or these airliners carrying their human cargo in air-conditioned cabins, pampered with custom armchairs, pillows, private video screens, fax machines and double martinis. Barely 80 years after she became the first American woman to earn her pilot's license, these things are a reality. Yet her vision went beyond that of the men in her day. She predicted the day would come when women would earn their livelihood from flying. Her vision was to most people in Victorian America a mere delusion, fantasy, or for some, a vague threat.

The mystique of flying has long captured our imagination. In 1751, a shipwrecked sailor met and married a woman named Youwarkee. The woman was unique. She could fly! In fact, all the members of her race possessed the ability to fly. Each had a special silky skin called a "graundee," that when spread created a set of wings. The sailor was mesmerized by Youwarkee's ability to fly and asked her to share her special talent. She said, "If you had but the graundee, flying would rest you, after the greatest labour . . . once you are upon the graundee at a proper height, all the rest is play, a mere trifle; you need only to think of your way, and incline to it, your graundee directs you as readily as your feet obey you on the ground without thinking of every step you take; it does not require labour, as your boat does, to keep you a-going."[1]

More than a hundred and fifty years later, when human flight was a reality, Gertrude Bacon described the sensation:

The ground was very rough and hard as we tore along, at an increasing pace that was very soon greater than any motorcar I had ever been in. I expected to be jerked and jolted. But suddenly there had come a new, indescribable quality - a lightness - a life! The motion was wonderfully smooth. There are many who know that feeling: that glorious, gliding sense that the sea bird has known these million years, which man so long and so vainly has envied, which now, familiarity can never rob of its charm.[2]

Gertrude Bacon wrote these words after her first airplane ride in 1909, to express the exhilaration shared by every pilot. While she was only a passenger in the airplane, Gertrude represented a new and privileged class of people who could detach themselves from the bounds of earth and experience flight. She was also the first British woman to ride in a dirigible. Both the pilot and Gertrude were brave souls. Aviation was in its infancy and the progress of a successful flight was measured in minutes. Air crashes which usually involved only one person got the same notoriety as they do today.

The pilots who followed Gertrude Bacon into the air would experience the same freedom from the confines of gravity. They all would experience risk-taking inherent in early flight and some would experience the sudden death that came from the unstable, flimsy wood and canvas contraptions. Finally, many would also share the experience of loneliness and the prejudice of their contemporaries. Sadly, those who suffered those negative experiences were mostly women.

In general most women did not dare fly. Such an act would break the prevailing standard of proper etiquette and decorum for the "fair sex." Increasing numbers of women in the United States had been defying the social norms. Women were driving the new motor cars and engaging in some masculine non-contact sports, such as target shooting, golf, and a carefully paced game of tennis. There were women who knew instinctively they could fly an airplane as well as a man, and, like all the hopeful aviators of the times, had little or no formal instruction. Because of the social norms, however, the women would need more determination and enthusiasm than their male counterparts if they were to succeed.

European Aviation

In Europe, women's roles had evolved differently. In 1789, a few years after Joseph and Etienne Montgolfier launched their balloon, Madame Thibaud thrilled Paris with her balloon flights. Soon other French women began ballooning, and their fellow countrymen began worrying about the safety of their women. The chief of police of Paris said, "Women could not possibly stand the strain of riding in balloons."[3] He thought women should be protected from the temptations to fly. By the time King Louis XV was born in 1834, there were 22 European women who had piloted balloons. One French woman, Sophie Blanchard, became so skilled at balloon flying that Napoleon made her his air service chief.

Aviation in America

It took almost 36 years from the date the first French woman went aloft until the first American ventured into the air. A reporter for the *New York Evening Post* wrote an article in that newspaper in 1825 that "Mrs. Johnson" had successfully made a balloon ascent from New York City, landing finally in the Flatlands in what was then the city of Brooklyn. The next and more thoroughly recorded event of a woman going aloft occurred in 1855, when Miss Lucretia Bradley flew in a balloon from Easton, Pennsylvania to Phillipsburg, New Jersey.

The first American woman credited with piloting her own balloon billed herself as "Carlotta, the Lady Astronaut." Her real name was Mary H. Myers, of Mohawk, New York. See This flight took place on July 4, 1880 at Little Falls, New York. She became famous by setting an altitude record of more than 20,000 feet in a balloon filled with natural gas. This achievement was notable, but Mary also ascended to more than 20,000 feet without the benefit of supplemental oxygen.

More than a hundred years passed after the first intrepid French women ventured into the air before there were any significant improvements in air travel. The evolution of aviation moved slowly until the birth of the 20th

Century. Furthermore, until the Wright brothers' victory over gravity in 1903, ballooning remained the principal method of air travel, and it was mostly sport flying for those brave enough to challenge the unpredictable winds. On July 9, 1903, five months before the Wright brothers made their historic flight, a beautiful Cuban-American, Aida de Acosta soloed in a dirigible owned by the famous Brazilian dirigible designer Alberto Santos-Dumont. Aida de Acosta did not publicize her flight and upon landing on an active polo field, shocked players and spectators alike. The crowd expected to see a male pilot alight from the craft. The press severely criticized Santos-Dumont, and de Acosta's parents were so sickened by the offensive publicity that they made Santos-Dumont promise never to reveal the identity of their daughter. The history-making trip of Miss de Acosta faded like a sunset into the dark recesses of history, but that did not stop other women from flying. In 1906, Mary Miller became the first American-born woman to fly in a dirigible. Her pilot was a balloon designer and pilot, A. Leo Stevens.

Perhaps, given the early involvement of the women of France, it is fitting that another Frenchwoman, Baroness Raymonde de la Roche, would earn the title of the first woman in the world to earn her pilot's license. (Only two years earlier she had flown her first solo flight.) This was accomplished in 1910, just seven years after the Wright brothers had conquered flight in a heavier-than-air machine.

The Twentieth Century & American Women

American women fought to realize their dream of flight as well as their desire for freedom to vote and be accepted as equals. Their flying dreams would stand up to the test of time, endurance and determination. Flying was expensive and less than five million American women worked outside the home, with almost one-fourth of them in factories. Seventy-five percent of the working women were less than 25 years old, and were considered temporary workers. Marriage and a family would soon force them from the workplace. Women had even greater obstacles in aviation. If women stated their intentions to become involved in aviation, as passengers in a balloon or an airplane, they were ignored. Even public encouragement of their sons or husbands was often countered with anything from a mild personal rebuff to severe public censure. If the suggestion of women becoming pilots arose, it was whispered among women only.

Some women, recognizing the limitations society placed on them made contributions to aviation in other ways. Miss E. Lillian Todd, a secretary, was the first woman to design an airship and an airplane. While the airplane did not have an engine and did not fly, the airship did fly. Several newspapers of the day carried stories of encouragement from some notables such as respected aviator Alberto Santos-Dumont and philanthropist Andrew Carnegie. However, broad public or government encouragement was rare.

In 1908, six American women in Canton, Ohio, made a number of balloon flights with balloonist A. Leo Stevens. A few of the women wrote articles in contemporary magazines about their experiences. They were the exceptions to the rule, and their accomplishments also faded into obscurity.

Women in aviation were so rare in the early days that every "first" was recorded. The first American woman passenger to fly in a heavier-than-air machine was Mrs. Hart O. Berg, wife of the Wright brothers' European sales representative. See Fig. 1-1. The two minute, three-second flight took place at Auvers, France, in 1908. The first woman in America to fly as an airplane passenger was Mrs. Ralph Van Deman, a good friend of Katharine Wright, the sister of the famous brothers. See Fig. 1-2.

By 1909, Geneve Shaffer of San Francisco was regularly piloting free balloons on the West coast. During one of her flights, she made the first aerial photographs of San Francisco and Oakland. Geneve was also the first woman to fly a glider. She made her solo glider flight on August 1, 1909.

The woman to have the distinction of being the first woman on a regularly scheduled airline was Mrs. L.A. Whitney, wife of the Secretary of Commerce of St. Petersburg, Florida. She made the trip on January 8, 1914, from St. Petersburg to Tampa, in a Benoist (pronounced "Ben Wa") flying boat. The speedy, 23 mile, 18 minute flight overshadowed the fact that a woman had flown across the bay. There was light coverage of Mrs. Whitney's ride and heavy coverage of the possibilities of aviation in Florida. The flight, however, was not without incident. The pilot, Tony Jannus, was forced to land the aircraft on Tampa bay, some distance from shore. Pilots being versatile mechanics in those days, he repaired the trouble and successfully completed the flight.

The most unusual "flight" for anyone, male or female, in those early days of aviation was made by Helen Mallard, of St. Louis, Missouri. She sat on a swing-like seat attached to 12 large kites. The contraption remained tethered, but rose about 40 feet before returning her to safety on the ground. The publicity stunt perpetrated by her husband accomplished little.

By 1911, any woman attempting to fly with a man in an airplane became instantly notorious. A rumor was circulating at the New York *Times* that someone had seen an unbelievable event, a woman taking flying lessons! A reporter from the *Times* hurried to the alleged location to see for himself if this rumor was true. This would make headline news, the reporter thought.

The veteran newsman walked slowly through the early morning mist engulfing the landing field at Garden City, Long Island. He moved closer with uncertainty - not sure of what to expect. His footsteps pressed the small pebbles along the path creating a muffled but audible crunching sound. A light breeze mixed a hint of the nearby Atlantic Ocean with the blooming honeysuckle bushes. A still-dark and silhouetted shape of the airplane hangar began to appear. The sun was rising slowly and the combination of mist and first light had cast an ethereal red glow on the landscape. Suddenly the hangar doors began to open. The reporter stopped in his tracks. Five shadowy figures emerged from the warm glow of the lighted interior. They were pushing a single-seat Bleriot-styled monoplane out of its protective cocoon. A sixth figure, the reporter noticed, walked behind the right wing of the machine.

The five men only paused momentarily when they saw the reporter, then continued pushing the monoplane past him. The sixth figure did not pause, but continued walking past the reporter. In the half-light of dawn, the reporter strained, trying to identify this figure who wore a regular pilot's ensemble: leather jacket, trousers, leather

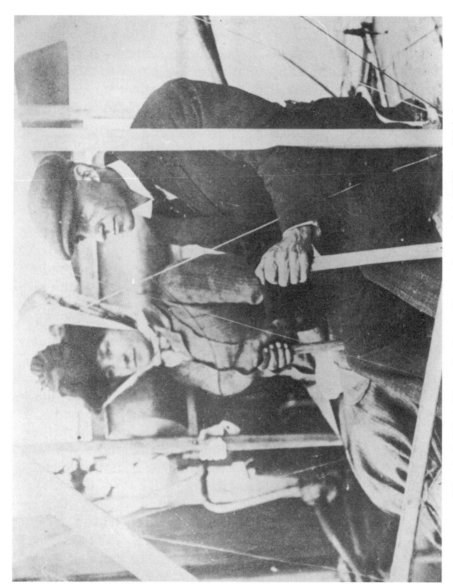

Fig. 1-1, Mrs. Hart O. Berg shown here with Wilbur Wright

puttees, heavy goggles and gloves. The outfitted figure walked lightly and was a bit on the thin side. A dark hood covered the pilot's face. That was odd, he thought. A breeze arose then and played with the fabric, pushing it off the person's forehead. The reporter gasped and recognized the well-known and definitely feminine features of Harriet Quimby, the drama critic for the well-regarded publication *Leslie's Illustrated Weekly*. She smiled a warm, radiant smile at the reporter, who stood with his mouth agape. All he could think of was, "What a story!" He was right, and it made the front page: "Woman in Trousers - Daring Aviator." Now America too had its first woman pilot, and people were not sure how to handle this new phenomenon.

Harriet Quimby and Family - The Early Years

Harriet Quimby was a popular figure in early aviation, and yet the few historical records of her life are filled with a series of contradictions and controversies. There were several mysteries around her life and her death. Some said she was born to wealth in Boston in 1884, others say she was born on an orange plantation in Arroyo Grande, California. One story said she attended private schools in the United States and in Europe. The application of modern aviation science has solved the mystery of her death and well-documented research has solved the riddle of where and when she was born.

William Quimby, the son of Irish immigrants, was of medium build with a long, brooding face. His skin, although exposed to weather, was usually milky white. His deeply rooted brown hair was thick, turbulent and stood in all directions from a line far down on his forehead. Quimby's blue eyes set deep and at a strange angle, seemed to turn their gaze inward. He married Ursula Cook, in Branch County, in Coldwater, Michigan, on October 9, 1859. Their marriage certificate shows Ursula Cook to be from Niagara, New York. Ursula Quimby was almost her husband's height, with tiny deep green eyes that seemed to catch the light and twinkle. Her face, had darkened with a blush of fullbloodedness from the years of working in the field. Her hair was silky black and remained young-looking

Fig. 1-2, Mrs Ralph Van Deman

years after the rest of her body began to succumb to harsh physical labor.

William was 30 years old in 1864, when he volunteered for the Union Army. A limp from a childhood injury kept him off the front lines for the year he spent in the service. He worked as the regimental cook with the 188th Infantry from New York. (In 1893, the government judged Quimby 100 percent disabled, and awarded him veteran's pension of $12 a month for the rest of his life.) After the war he and Ursula decided to begin their family. Their first daughter, Kittie, was born in 1870. Five years later and just past his 41st birthday his daughter Harriet was born on a farm in Ovid township, a few miles southwest of Coldwater, Michigan, on May 11, 1875.[4]

Harriet and her family apparently did not live long in Coldwater, for the 1880 government census finds them in Manistee County, in Michigan. Young Harriet Quimby is listed in the census as five years old. Her older sister Kittie is listed as ten. Four years later, William and Ursula Quimby moved their family to Arroyo Grande, California, a small farming community between Los Angeles and San Francisco. Moving a family halfway across the country in those days was not easy. Quimby and his wife had to pack all the earthly belongings they could carry and traveled to Lansing to catch a train to Chicago. Then they boarded the Union Pacific Railroad traveling to San Francisco, California. They got off at Oakland, and then had to board a stagecoach for a dusty ride to Arroyo Grande.

Arroyo Grande records show that the Quimbys owned a small farm in the San Luis Obispo area. After his farm failed, William took a job with the Steel brothers, who had a large dairy farm operation nearby. At this point there are conflicting stories about the Quimby family. Some early writers say William Quimby was a Charter Member of the local Odd Fellows Lodge # 258. The Lodge's charter shows a date of May 9, 1877, some seven years before Quimby and his family arrived in Arroyo Grande. That would also put this William Quimby in California three years before the census of 1880, which shows him living in Michigan. The Odd Fellows Lodge, however, does not have him listed as a member on the charter, and this is possibly part of an elaborate story later concocted by Ursula, his wife.

Fig. 1-3, Harriet Quimby, another "Gibson Girl"

Harriet's mother Ursula had a profound effect on her youngest daughter. Harriet spent her formative years being molded by the personality of her mother. Ursula Quimby was a firm believer in women's emancipation and Harriet was to later emulate her mother's convictions. It was her mother's teaching and coaching that enabled Harriet to enter the 20th century and fulfill her destiny.

Ursula Quimby decided her daughters would not grow up depending on a man for their food or their basic survival, and they would not perform the backbreaking fast-aging work required of a farmer. The years of 14-hour days working on the farm had taken a physical toll on Ursula. William had worked sporadically and generally unsuccessfully at various jobs. The 1890s were financially unstable times in America with bank failures and financial panics. William Quimby tried to run a general store after his farm failed but the store also failed. It was then that Ursula Quimby took control of her family's destiny. She convinced her husband to move to San Francisco where jobs were more plentiful and the economy more stable. Harriet's uncle, her mother's brother, was renowned for herbal medicine cures. Harriet and her mother set up a cottage industry mixing and bottling the herbal remedies. Meanwhile, William became an itinerant salesman selling the curatives from a wagon. Ursula Quimby and her daughters augmented the family's income by making prune sacks for the local fruit-packing industry and this enabled Ursula to send her daughters to the better schools in the city.

Ursula, however, was disappointed when her daughter Kittie married and left home with her husband to start a new life. Harriet, on the other hand, was still young enough to mold into a strong and independent woman.

Harriet Quimby - Working Woman

To prepare young Harriet to cope with the male-dominated society, her mother began an image-building campaign. She told people Harriet was born in 1884, making her nine years younger than she really was. She also created a fantasy life for Harriet by telling people Harriet was born in Boston and schooled in Switzerland and France. There was a Quimby family in Boston at the time, and it is entirely possible that William, although a New Yorker, was related to them. Her father, as one story goes, was a member of the United States Consulate Service, and a collector of rare English silverware. Ursula felt this younger, well-educated, supposedly affluent image, would enhance Harriet's acceptance as a woman of intelligence, bearing, and independence. Harriet excelled in the local public schools, and it was not difficult for her mother to invent the image of her daughter as a well-educated young woman. Ursula steered Harriet toward a singular goal: to be a journalist. Journalism was a field opening more to women, and Ursula Quimby thought it would give her daughter prominent exposure and lead to meeting the "right people."

Harriet was 25 years old in 1900, and is listed with her mother and father in the 1900 census of San Francisco, but her sister Kittie had moved from the home and thereafter was lost to history. By the age of 26, Harriet had found work with the San Francisco *Dramatic Review* and later she worked for the *Call-Bulletin & Chronicle* and wrote Sunday features for that paper. Determined to become a good reporter, young Harriet would search for stories around the city, write them, and hand them to her editor. She had a strong determination to succeed as a reporter and soon the editor, Will Irwin, remarked that Harriet had the "best nose for news" he had ever seen. Soon he began to give her regular assignments. Quimby quickly began to build a reputation in the industry as one of the *Chronicle's* best reporters. In time, her byline became well-known in northern California.

One of Harriet's earliest contributions to the *Chronicle* appeared in the February 2, 1902 issue. Entitled "A Night At A Haunted House," this well-written fiction was not typical of her writing, which was primarily non-fiction. She did hold a dream of someday writing fiction, but she found nonfiction paid the bills. (Another invented story surrounding Harriet Quimby's life is that she wanted to use flying to become independently wealthy by the age of 35, and then turn to her first love, creative writing. In fact, she did not see her first airplane until she was 35.) Her talent for writing was to take an ordinary story and transform it into an armchair adventure for her readers. She would explore the streets of San Francisco and record its sights, sounds, and smells so her readers experienced the same journey. Quimby was constantly drawn to the city's Chinatown, where she found an inexhaustible source of material in its inhabitants and customs.

Harriet Quimby soon became known for her intelligence, vivaciousness, charm, and sense of humor. Doors that would otherwise be closed to a reporter, especially in Chinatown, were open to her. This lively style was conveyed also in her writing.

Harriet Quimby, by all accounts and photographs, was a strikingly beautiful woman. She had inherited the fair complexion and jet black hair of her mother, and the blue eyes of her father. In an interview in *World Magazine*, the reporter said she had a "brilliant smile, and she runs strongly to overhung bonnets and antique ornaments . . . so that even in business attire her individuality is very distinctive." This description belies the facts. Her photos show her in plain-styled dresses, never in overhung bonnets, and the only antique ornaments she wore were a necklace and bracelet, which she considered her good luck charms. Yet there is no doubt Harriet's individuality was clear. Her smile was luminous, and her blue, sometimes greenish eyes were scintillating. Her smile displayed her only obvious physical flaw. Barely perceptible in some of her photographs is evidence of repaired chipped front teeth. This did not in any way detract from her beauty. This glamorous young journalist soon became admired in society circles. She became an acknowledged beauty in the age of the "Gibson Girl" and her portrait hung in the all-male Bohemian Club until the club and its artwork crumbled in the great San Francisco earthquake of 1906.[5] See Fig. 1-3.

In later years, after she became an aviation personality, reporters asked Harriet why she had chosen to be a journalist. She replied, "Why I just began to write. I always had a taste that way, and when I went to San Francisco I began working for the Sunday editions of the papers there. Occasionally I got things into the magazines, but the greater part of my writing was the sort people lump under the general title of newspaper work."[6]

Harriet was not a feminist, yet believed in women's rights and individuality. She believed strongly in women's right to vote but she was not enthusiastic about the Suffrage movement. She thought their tactics were inflammatory and adversarial. Harriet believed as her mother did in the emancipation of women from the Victorian lifestyle that followed them into the 20th Century. Whenever possible, her articles were filled with tips on how women could find safe and inexpensive lodging, jobs, and improve themselves. Word of Harriet's talent reached the East coast, and soon there were inquires about Miss Quimby's availability to relocate. She saw the potential of working in New York and decided to make the move.

Harriet Quimby had reached adulthood at a time in American society when a young woman of good family and education, (the things Harriet's mother had fictionalized for her daughter) looked forward to an early marriage and family responsibilities. Harriet, however, did not shock her mother when she announced plans to move East and make her mark as a journalist. The young woman was consumed by her ambitions and did not let any serious or permanent romantic attachments interfere with her career, as it was difficult enough convincing narrow-minded editors to take her seriously; any hint of marriage would have immediately ended any career hopes.

The New York Years

It was a cold day in early January 1903, when Harriet arrived in the smoke-filled corridors of Pennsylvania Station. The size of the terminal was intimidating. It seemed to tower toward the sky. Steel columns rose from track level to well over one hundred feet. The immense arched glass ceiling cascaded sunlight to the floor below. Eerie, filtered sabers of light, tinted with grey clouds of smoke, drifted from the tunnels and up into the station.

Quimby climbed the steel stairs from the track platform to the main level of the terminal. She looked up. The great clock over the entrance showed five minutes past twelve. Steel girders supporting the ceiling looked like part of a bridge. Quimby suspected Mr. Eiffel of the French tower fame had an influence on the architect. She then looked backwards and noticed two things. There was a third rail in the track roadbed below, and she knew it carried electricity for the train. She wondered when they had switched from the coal-burning engine, and why there was so much smoke in the station. The other thing she noticed was the steel picket fence, the only protection against falling to the tracks below. The openness of the station above her was a contrast to the crowded floor area.

When she got her bearings she saw a sign, "Main Waiting Room and Red Cap Service." She climbed a flight of white marble stairs finding herself in a great vaulted hall. This room was more cavernous than the one she had just left. Instead of steel girders, there now were six massive white marble Corinthian columns on each wall. This was surely a vision out of ancient Rome in its finest hour, she thought.

The terminal was crowded with people. There were dozens of people just milling around waiting for friends and relatives or trains, and would-be travelers rushing every which way. It reminded her of the chaos of a fishbowl with fish going in all directions.

The great hall was well-lit with sunshine but Harriet wondered if the seven-bulb chandeliers that hung from the 200-foot ceiling provided enough light at night. As she stood in amazement of the terminal's size it occurred to Harriet that on her first day in New York City she knew no one, had no idea of how to get around the city, where to live, or where to look for a job. Those obstacles did not intimidate or deter the young woman. She had left her job in San Francisco on good terms with the editor. And she had a standing offer from him that there was always a job waiting for her should she decide to return home. Harriet knew the value of not burning her bridges. A bulletin board inside the station advertised boarding houses and apartments, however, she had been warned before she left San Francisco to not venture downtown looking for a place to live. Even at the turn of the century, New York City had its pockets of crime, and bad neighborhoods where an unescorted single woman was a potential target. Luckily, her former editor had given Harriet a friend's name who lived in New York as a contact. The next day she would call her. Meanwhile, she would stay at the Pennsylvanian Hotel. She stopped at the marble desk in the main concourse of the terminal to ask directions to the hotel. The courteous clerk directed her toward a

Fig. 1-4, Harriet Quimby

long flight of marble stairs. Quimby then collected her two steamer trunks of luggage, enlisted a Red Cap and braced to meet the unexpected beyond the great marble hall. With a Red Cap pulling her luggage, she climbed the stairs to the street. Almost immediately she was flanked by men offering carriage service. She smiled politely, declining their invitation. Now the Red Cap led the way across the cobblestone street to the hotel directly across from the station. The street she noticed was awful. Horse droppings were everywhere, and there were puddles of water and sheets of dirty ice between her and the hotel. She smiled to herself. This city was going to be a challenge, she thought.

After she checked in, the bellboy led her through the spacious lobby and toward the newly installed electric elevator. When the bellboy arrived at the elevator he turned and noticed his guest was still in the main lobby. Harriet was standing off to one side admiring the crystal chandeliers, absorbing the richness of the mahogany wood columns and the exquisite paintings that adorned the walls. Elderly gentlemen sat in deep-piled armchairs smoking cigars and reading newspapers. She wondered briefly if they were employed or wealthy tycoons. Some of them reminded her of the Vanderbilts and the Morgans.

When she noticed the bellboy waiting she nodded graciously and walked to the elevator. Harriet was keenly perceptive and the writer in her was absorbing every sight and sound. She had an acute sense of detail and was aware of everything going on around her. The elevator door was distinctive from the rest of the lobby motif. Its large shiny brass door was embellished with kaleidoscope designs, trimmed with copper. Before she could absorb all it had to offer, the door opened. The bellboy gestured for her to step in first. The elevator operator greeted Quimby with a pleasant smile and closed the outer door. He then closed the steel accordion-like gate. He looked at the bellboy who in turn held up his hand and extended four gloved fingers. The operator nodded acknowledgement, smiled at Quimby and pushed the lever that operated the electric motor. The small box-like compartment rose slowly. Quimby watched quietly as the plane brick wall of the shaft crept by, broken only by the plain side of the door to each floor.

After unpacking a few toiletries Quimby checked the bath closet down the hall. It was not occupied. Now she could take a sorely missed tub bath. The five days on the sooty train had left her skin and clothes in desperate need of cleansing. She did not, however, like the idea of bathing in a hotel bathtub. She was used to her own private bath back in San Francisco.

Only after she had locked the door to the bath closet did Quimby settle into the steamy hot water and relax. The water quickly produced a dream-like state and Harriet reflected on some of the hotel clerk's remarks. Of course she had travelled across the country unescorted, she replied to the surprised hotel clerk. "You're just staying one night?" was another seemingly accusatory question. She remembered the clerk looking over her steamer trunks before shrugging his shoulders. At the time she had not given much thought to these questions. After all they seemed innocent enough. Now upon reflection she knew the clerk had his own opinion of her probable occupation. Only when she told him that she was a journalist and produced a letter of reference from her former editor did the clerk's demeanor change - a little. She remembered too that his look made her uncomfortable. So this is New York City, she thought. One had to learn quickly how to come up with answers and solutions to all sorts of predicaments and misunderstandings. She then decided that she would have her dinner delivered to her room.

Looking For Work

The next day, she used the hotel lobby phone to phone her contact. With her assistance Quimby found accommodations in a rooming house on Third Avenue, on the upper East side of Manhattan at 68th Street. The one room was small, but it faced Third Avenue and the elevated train tracks. Her two windows facing East were large, but cloaked with heavy draperies, typical of the period. Harriet immediately swept them aside allowing in plenty of daylight and fresh air. The first train of the morning would rumble by at five a.m. and serve as her alarm clock. Sunrise would greet her in the morning and the afternoon shade would cool the tiny apartment in the summer. She was on the fourth floor and her view was level with the train tracks. There was a fire escape on the window which served as an outdoor refrigerator during the winter. If she did not feel like going to the kitchen on her floor she shared with five other guests on that floor she could keep a bottle of milk and a few other items cool and make herself a snack in the privacy of her own room. In the summertime it would be a different story.

The rent, which included two meals daily, was three dollars and fifty cents a week. This was somewhat expensive considering that in 1903, the New York *Times* (22 pages) cost one cent, eggs were 14 cents a dozen, and men's suits were ten dollars. However, the building had the convenience of in-room plumbing. America was growing; indoor plumbing had brought together in one room the toilet from the outhouse, the washbowl from the bedchamber and the bathtub from the kitchen. Harriet's neighbors were hardworking Irish and German immigrants, and with her looks and name they made her feel right at home.

The next morning Quimby set out looking for a job. The air had the scent of malt and she enjoyed the smell even though she was puzzled by its origin. She would later learn that one of the city's largest breweries was nearby. The streets uptown were filled with a dirty black slush, the reminder of last week's snowstorm. The hem of Harriet's skirt, weighted with lead like all women's skirts in those days, quickly became soggy and soiled as she walked toward the trolley car. Showing the female ankle in 1903 was considered bad taste, so women wore long skirts and covered their lower legs with cotton or lisle. (Only 12,000 pairs of silk stockings were manufactured in the United States that year and only the wealthy could afford them.[7]) This city was not like San Francisco, she thought. Her first impressions of New York were not good, but Harriet would reserve her judgement on the city until she had spent more time there. The newspaper offices were downtown, near City Hall in a section of the city called "Printing Press Row," so the young reporter braved the rush hour crowds to get to Park Place. She had been used to the open-air trolleys of San Francisco, the enclosed trolley cars on Third Avenue beneath the elevated train tracks were a different story. She had never seen people being treated like cattle on public transportation! And she had never been squeezed into a trolley car and crushed like this in San Francisco. It caused her to think she may like the diversity of this city. But she would have to learn how to deal with the crowds.

By the time Harriet got off the streetcar at City Hall, she was a bit ruffled. However, her spirits were still high, and she began making the rounds of the newspapers with some of her published material. Harriet also had the foresight to write a few articles in the week it took her to cross the country. The young professional hoped that she would be able to use them to bring in some money until she landed a full-time job.

The editors of the New York papers were a tough bunch, only looking for results, and they were also skeptical of a female reporter. There were not many women journalists in 1903 but fortunately most of them were on the East coast. Women had been involved in journalism for well over 150 years when Quimby came along, but they had maintained a very low profile outside the journalism community. The general public and many of the journalists of Quimby's day had no idea that Ann Franklin, sister-in-law to Benjamin Franklin, was a writer and had operated a publishing house in 1735. She had taken over her husband James' press after he died and was extremely capable. Within a year of her husband's death she was appointed Colony Printer by the King of England. She produced printing for the Crown and several books. Ann Franklin was one of many women who worked in the printing and publishing trade in the colonies, carrying on a tradition well established in England and Europe as early as the 16th century when women were well-known in printing, publishing and bookselling. The Company of Stationers' records listed more than 60 women printers in England alone. With the Industrial Revolution, and the growth of the cities, the numbers of women in the publishing field in the United States slowly dwindled as men began accumulating the wealth and starting publishing houses.[8] At *Leslie's Illustrated Weekly*, Frank Leslie's widow continued publication after his death and ran it successfully for many years.

Quimby would in the final analysis be judged on what she could produce from her pen, and editors were mildly interested in what the reporter had written and published in the past but more interested in her potential to make money for their newspapers. The assistant editor at *Leslie's Illustrated Weekly* (later called *Leslie's Weekly*) first interviewed her. He was impressed with her published material but Quimby detected a reluctance on his part to make a decision. She was right. He passed her on to the associate editor. He too was impressed, but said the decision was with the editor who was not in. "Come back tomorrow," he said.

The next day she showed up at the editor's office at 7:45 a.m. That should impress him, she thought. It did. He invited her in and even poured her a cup of coffee which she dared not touch for fear he would see her hand shaking from nerves.

After he had reviewed her published work and that which she had written on the train trip he began a critique. "I would not have said this that way," he proclaimed as he read a paragraph out loud. "I would have said," and he proceeded to reword the entire paragraph. He then looked over at Quimby and said, "See what I mean?" Quimby nodded graciously and smiled. Inside she was burning. She felt like saying, "I got it published, and someone paid me for it, didn't they?" But again, discretion was the better part of valor and she remained silent.

Finally he began interviewing her in terms of trying her out on a few assignments, and then he had second thoughts. He reread one of her articles and decided out loud that Harriet was not a literary genius. He then suggested she might consider another line of work. Harriet smiled warmly at him when he had finished his verbal assault on her work, then replied that was precisely the same opinion she held of herself. However, she said, she had tried cooking and felt she could write better than she could cook. The young woman then went on to tell him that the two of them would get along fine. The editor was so taken by her reply, that he hired her on the spot as a part-time freelance writer. The year was 1903 and later that year two brothers on a beach in North Carolina would change the course of human history and seal the destiny and fate of Harriet Quimby. See Fig. 1-4.

The young beauty had come East with a different perspective on a woman's place in society. Her mother's rearing and the more liberated life of the women in the West provided an emancipated perspective. All of this came at a time when universal suffrage was almost two decades away and there would be years of turmoil before the issue would be nationally resolved. For example, women in Wyoming were the first in the nation to win the right to vote in state elections, in 1869. Yet writer George Bernard Shaw pessimistically predicted, ". . . give women the vote and in five years there would be a crushing tax on bachelors."

The editor had taken a chance on Harriet. Her first article appeared on January 22, 1903 issue of *Leslie's Illustrated Weekly*. The piece titled, "Curious Chinese Customs" convinced the editor she had talent. It also reflected her continuing curiosity with America's melting-pot culture, and social issues. After a trial period of approximately one year, Harriet so impressed her editor with her journalism skills that he promoted her to a full-time position at the paper and by 1906, she was their resident drama critic. Again, Quimby had to "encourage" the editor toward that decision by attending the theater and doing mock reviews which she submitted to him. The work was good, and after the editor had published five of her reviews, the praise was coming in. Quimby was lauded for her fair and comprehensive coverage. It was the consistent high quality of her work that convinced the editor to hire Harriet both as drama critic and editor of the Women's Page.

Once on the staff full-time, Quimby decided to take another bold step. All of the full-time reporters were men, and they were using a new mechanical device called a typewriter. Once she saw how fast a story could be written with a typewriter Harriet set out to learn how to use the machine. This of course upset her colleagues but their displeasure soon subsided. Those who knew Harriet Quimby knew that a few unhappy people would not slow her down or dissuade her. She was not a person who felt guilty for other people's actions or behavior. The resistance was short-lived because there were opinions developing that women had a particular aptitude to using a typewriter and operating a switchboard.

It did not take long for Harriet to discover the severe drawbacks of living in a boarding house. It was small, cramped, and people were always moving in and out. Mud was constantly being tracked through the rooms due to construction of a subway in the area and last but not least were the rodents and cockroaches. She would make do, however, and resigned herself for the present, until she had saved enough to move into a good hotel. She set a goal that within six months she would move into a bigger and less expensive place. During this period, the young writer also met and befriended several other women working for newspapers and soon exchanged invitations with them for lunch or tea on the weekends. This new-found social calendar fueled her enthusiasm and soon brightened her life. Living in New York had at last begun to be fun.

Six months later, between her theater reviews for *Leslie's Illustrated Weekly* and her freelance assignments, Harriet had saved enough money to move into the Hotel Victoria on 27th Street and Broadway. The eight-story building had the "latest plunger-type hydraulic elevator - the safest - and best in the world." And the rates were reasonable, from $1.50 per week. At this time, she also moved her aging mother East to live with her. Her father remained in California, still searching for his place in life.

The atmosphere in New York City was contagious, and Harriet found life in New York City exciting. Its wide variety of culture, Chinatown, Little Italy, Yorktown (where the German and Irish immigrants lived), the tenements of Delancy Street and the immigrants coming through Ellis Island, rivaled San Francisco for great sources of stories. There was the suburban atmosphere of Brooklyn, and the farms on Long Island. It was not long before Harriet discovered a gold mine of story material. She soon became a regular freelance contributor to many city newspapers and magazines.

Quimby loved to travel, and as a self-proclaimed liberated woman, she often traveled unescorted. From a vacation trip to Cuba in 1906, she wrote and had published almost a dozen stories. After this trip she earned a promotion. She became *Leslie's Illustrated Weekly's* first travel correspondent. The job took her to Egypt, South America, and Africa. She even published exotic recipes that she collected in her travels, encouraging her women readers to try new things. Harriet Quimby captivated people with her beauty, and sometimes shocking them with her behavior. On one of her trips to Europe, she learned to use a camera and supplemented her stories with photographs. Not many people had seen women using mechanical devices like a camera. Quimby had everybody buzzing with excitement once their shock wore off.

In the early 20th Century, the horse and carriage were still considered the mark of elegance, but the automobile was creating a new social class. One day, Harriet Quimby went to an auto race on Long Island, and managed to convince one race driver to take her around the track in his racing car. Harriet's heart pounded, and the 60 mph speed in the open car nearly took her breath away. This was her first taste of danger associated with speed and Harriet Quimby found it intoxicating. From that moment on automobiles drew the young woman like a magnet. She quickly penned an article from that singular experience, entitled "A Woman's Exciting Ride in a Motor Car."[9]

One racing car experience and the catharsis of writing about it did not cure Harriet of the fever. She then took another bold step for a woman in 1906: she found someone who would give her driving lessons. The young writer obtained her driver license bought a car and after that drove to her writing assignments.

Dawn of A New Era For Women

By 1911, there was noticeable change in women's access to automobiles. Harriet Quimby wrote an article in *Leslie's Weekly* pointing out the changes that had taken place. "It is no longer a novel sight to see a slender young girl piloting a powerful runabout through the congested traffic of a city's busy streets, or a heavy touring car guided by a feminine hand. Milady has come to the conclusion that 'carburetor trouble' is just as fashionable as appendicitis and a great deal more enjoyable."[10]

Quimby discussed the automobile "academies" opening up around the city and how some were admitting women. "If husbands, fathers and brothers could look in while a class is in session, they would be amazed. They would find their dainty and fastidious relatives with greasy hands and smudged faces. They would be hard at work setting the valves of an engine or changing the mixture of the carburetor. These women would also show the same amount of satisfaction that the average man shows in doing the work."[11] Quimby pointed out that in the past women had been victimized by unscrupulous mechanics. "Women who have taken this course know something about the running of an automobile and cannot be fooled by a chauffeur and charged for repairs that are not necessary."[12]

According to the driving academy's owner, women made superior drivers, better in fact than men. Quimby interviewed him and he boasted that his academy had taught "several hundred women in the last two years." He said, "Women as a rule are less nervous than men when learning to drive. None have ever been involved in an accident while in my school. That is not true for my male students. Another thing I have observed," he said, "is that women are more careful drivers than men to a point. When it comes to taking a risk, however, a woman will glide in and pass where a man will hesitate."

Quimby also mentioned that women had figured prominently in endurance tests and would not be surprised if she soon saw women drivers competing against men in speed tests. "Automobiles have opened up a new world for women. The tendency before the arrival of the motor car was to keep house and find most of her pleasures indoors. Now the automobile has drawn her into the open air. Money that formerly went to doctor bills is now well invested in the motor car and pink cheeks, sparkling eyes and the best of health are the result."[13]

Times were changing, but change, as always, met resistance. Every attempt at change or introduction of a new idea about evolving roles of women usually brought out strong opinions as to why things should remain the same. A woman's primary role was still to bear and nurture a large family. That responsibility overshadowed the other two secular interests that society dictated: husband and household. Women installed in their homes overstuffed and "gender distinctive" furniture, throne-like chairs for men, and armless, straight-back wooden chairs for women.

An editorial in *Leslie's Weekly* hinted at another sign of change. It described an attempt by a major hotel to introduce a "woman's bar," a small alcove in the main bar where women could go and "sip at a teeny weeny afternoon cocktail." The experiment apparently failed and the newspaper decided that "women still prefer a cup of afternoon tea to something stronger in the privacy of a woman's bar." The editorial concluded by saying it was a ". . . barometer of the times. Unfortunately," it said, "we have enough modern customs making inroads into the simplicity of life without adding a woman's bar to the list."[14]

The attempt to establish a "woman's bar" was just the tip of an iceberg that would melt slowly, too slowly for many women. Women in business and not in the home would soon become a major issue.

Another editorial in *Leslie's Weekly* sent mixed signals to women. Titled "Either Business or Home But Not Both," the editor began, "Is a woman naturally unsuited for the business world and does it age her prematurely?" From there it did not get any better. The editor described a doctor who claimed that women who worked farms were "worn out by thirty-five or forty" although she worked in a healthy outdoor environment. The editorial concluded that "Some women are naturally suited for some business positions and would find home duties more trying. Others would find just the reverse is the case. That a great change has taken place in public employment of women in very recent years is apparent to all. Women have entered the business field to stay. The important caution is that she should not try to fill a business position and run a home simultaneously. Such double work would be too much for any woman or even a man."[15]

Some women felt they had the right to compete with men in sports. But the men who influenced society and public opinion were out to dissuade them. Dr. Dudley Sargent, of Harvard University, publicly cautioned women against playing the usual male contact sports. "Let women," he said, "confine themselves to the lighter and more graceful forms of gymnastics and athletics. She should make herself superior this way as she has already done in aesthetic dancing. Let her know enough about the rougher sports to be the sympathetic admirer of men and boys in their efforts to be strong, vigorous and heroic."[16]

Some women were openly rebelling and usually suffered society's consequences. In 1908, Kate Mulcahey was arrested in New York for smoking a cigarette in public. This was a violation of the Sullivan Smoking Act, which prohibited such "unlady-like acts in public places." The judge fined her five dollars and sent her to jail over-night.[17]

As America industrialized, the need for a larger work force arose and women and children were looked upon as a source of cheap and plentiful labor. Women were not accepted into the mainstream of the business world but were exploited and hired to menial and underpaid jobs. On March 25, 1911 one of many industrial tragedies to befall women took place in New York. The Triangle Waist Company, a shirt making factory, had a fire that destroyed the interior of the building. In the heat and panic caused by the flames 146 women perished. Owners of the building had declared it to be fireproof and had built only one fire escape. The tragedy did raise public awareness as to unsafe factory conditions, but did not address the wages or sweat-shop conditions under which women worked. These harsh cir-cumstances and public attitudes gave Quimby fodder for her pen but she was about to test the endurance and commitment of the American male to his Victorian values in another way.

Chapter Two

The Statue of Liberty Race

"There were not many flying schools that would accept women. Goodness, they didn't want us driving motor cars, can you imagine airplanes?" - Matilde Moisant, 1911

Harriet Quimby's gregarious personality easily made her friends from all walks of life. One group she befriended was a small but eager gaggle of fledgling aviators. In the Fall of 1910, Miss Quimby, now 35, had gone to Belmont Park on Long Island at the invitation of her closest friend, Matilde Moisant. See Fig. 2-1. Quimby was excited to travel anywhere for a story, and was always looking for something dramatic to share with her readers. Horse-racing parks it turned out were natural aerodromes, and Belmont Park, on Long Island, in New York, became a choice spot for an air show. This was Harriet's first encounter with an airplane. Belmont Park had evolved with early aviation into the 1910 "Jet Set," and everyone who was anyone in society and aviation attended. Some saw the future of America and their future linked to this frail and shaky wooden vehicle. Others saw the event as a social gathering. The skies were filled indiscriminately with an assortment of biplanes, monoplanes, balloons and dirigibles, and more than a few people attended the air meet expecting to see a fiery crash. See Fig. 2-2. This was only America's second air show. The first had occurred in January, 1910, at Dominguez Field near Los Angeles. It had been an overwhelming success.

Quimby watched in amazement as the "birdmen-heroes" as she later called them, did loops and dives and posed for pictures in their biplanes and monoplanes. The event attracted 24 of the world's greatest pilots and included the elegant Englishman Claude Grahame-White, Frenchman Herbert Latham, and Americans Glenn Curtiss, Ralph Johnstone and Arch Hoxsey.

After seeing these odd-shaped contraptions in the sky, Miss Quimby concocted an angle for a story. It was October 30, the day before Halloween, and Quimby could link these odd-shaped machines screeching through the skies with the more traditional gremlins, ghosts, and goblins. Matilde told Quimby that her brother John was in an event - the air race. Now *that* sounded exciting to Harriet.

John Bevins Moisant was a self-promoting entrepreneur who had developed a reputation for being flamboyant. He had crashed an airplane on the first day of the show but walked away unhurt. (When the ten days of the event were over, Moisant had destroyed three machines and walked away from each wreck, further enhancing his self-proclaimed image of being the "King of Aviation.") Moisant had shocked his European contemporaries and the general public by displaying a cavalier attitude toward danger.

Quimby was not disappointed. The air race *was* exciting. Harriet witnessed Moisant, a wealthy investor, fly in a new monoplane from Belmont Park to the Statue of Liberty and back, 36 miles in a total air time of 34 minutes. He won the Statue of Liberty Race, defeating the best pilots Europe had to offer. At that air meet in Belmont Park, Moisant also came in second in the Schneider Cup race for float planes.

John Moisant had come to flying late in life through a succession of jobs, some legally questionable. He had been a farmer, sugar planter, banker, revolutionary (in Central America), and airplane designer. His last profession, that of an aviator-gentleman, is probably the one he is most remembered for, if he is remembered at all. This five foot eight-inch dapper gentleman formed the first flying circus in America. The air show sparked a fire for flying in Harriet's heart. "It really looks quite easy," she thought. "I believe I could do it myself, and I will."

Fig. 2-1, Matilde Moisant

Fig. 2-2, A poster announcing the Belmont Air Meet

From this event, Harriet decided that she too must eventually take up flying, and she shared this with Matilde. That evening the two women had dinner with the victorious John Moisant and a balloon pilot, A. Leo Stevens in the Hotel Astor. Stevens would later play an important role both in Harriet's life, both on a business and personal level. At Matilde's encouragement, Quimby told Moisant that she would like to learn to fly. Harriet then also volunteered Matilde as a candidate for flight instruction. It sounded like such fun that Matilde instantly agreed. John Moisant and his brother Alfred had opened the Moisant Aviation School in Hempstead, on Long Island, but he informed the two women that winter was too close to begin lessons. He also said he was going South to attend some air meets. He promised to teach them in the spring. "There were not many flying schools that would accept women," said Matilde. "Goodness, they didn't want us driving motor cars, can you imagine airplanes?" Her point was valid. When Orville Wright, one of the Wright brothers, first opened his flying school in Alabama, in 1910, he rejected all female applicants because he felt that they were just seeking notoriety. Although Katharine Wright was a great believer in the future of aviation and supported her brothers' efforts, Orville's attitude is most likely the reason she never learned to fly. (Under pressure from several women and seeing the potential revenue gains, Wright later opened his school to women.)

The winter sped by quickly for Harriet. Although not an active social reformer or feminist, Quimby stayed busy writing articles on the binding poverty, child labor, and industrial cruelty that scarred current and past generations of women and children in New York City. She attended new theater plays and wrote to friends in California. But she always kept her vision of the airplanes she had seen at Belmont Park foremost in her mind. Quimby had fallen in love with the monoplane shape. The simplicity of the design - like a bird, as opposed to the box-shaped and bulky biplanes - impressed Quimby.

Flying Lessons

In the spring, Quimby's passion for this new adventure had not faded. But a tragic event had taken place. In early January 1911, Harriet and her friend Matilde received word that Matilde's brother John died in an airplane accident near New Orleans, on December 31, 1910. For most people that would have ended plans to take flying lessons. Not for Harriet Quimby or Matilde Moisant! Although shaken by the death of his brother, Alfred decided not to close their flying school. Americans in aviation recognized that they were behind European aviation and Alfred Moisant said he wanted to ". . . raise aviation in the United States from its condition of stagnation or worse to the place it occupies abroad."[1] On May 10, Harriet and Matilde enrolled in Moisant's aviation school on Nassau Boulevard, on Long Island. They began their lessons the same day.

Matilde was one of five sisters and brothers and all but Alfred objected strongly to her need to fly. Quimby's father, who by this time had joined his wife in New York City, was also strongly against his daughter flying. "Women do not belong flying or in any other man's activity," he said. He knew, however, he was wasting his breath on his daughter. The loss of John in the flying accident had made them all cautious, but Harriet would not be dissuaded. She was thirty-five years old and although she loved her parents and respected them, but this was something she wanted to do. Ursula Quimby was apprehensive about anyone flying, however, she acquiesced to her daughter. After all, though it was dangerous, it was something a woman should have the right to pursue.

Because of the social pressures toward women in that period, the two women dressed disguised as men for their lessons. Harriet always took her lessons at sunrise. Then the lessons did not interfere with her work (and possible criticism or embarrassment for her employer), the air was usually calm, and she could keep her activities a secret - or so she thought. When a reporter discovered Harriet's charade, she was happy to see it end. The newspapers gave her much publicity. The press described Harriet as a "willowy brunette" and they quickly tagged her with the nickname "The Dresden China Aviatrix" because of her "beauty, daintiness, and haunting blue eyes." Quimby quickly became well-known, and almost notorious, but she was a strong woman. "Harriet enjoyed the publicity," said Matilde Moisant. See Fig. 2-3.

That day, Quimby informed her editor about her secret life as a student pilot, and the about-to-be-published article. Not surprising to her, he was delighted. Over the years they had developed a close professional relationship and he was well aware of Harriet's talents. He was surprised that she had decided to take up flying, though. It was at the time one of the most controversial topics in the country.

There was another reason that the editor greeted Harriet's news with enthusiasm. After all, here was a whole new angle for her to write about. There were aviation stories in the papers in those days, but most of the stories were about tragedies in the air. The editor recognized that he had a still-breathing aviation expert on his staff, and that would surely capture the public's fancy and increase readership. Only after the reporter from the *Times* let it be known that Quimby was taking flying lessons did the editor at *Leslie's Weekly* capitalize on the publicity generated by his most famous employee. The first official acknowledgement that Quimby had taken flying lessons came in a May 25, 1911 article in *Leslie's Weekly* entitled "How A Woman Learns To Fly." In a follow-up article on June 22, 1911, titled "Exploring the Air Lanes," her editor added this preface:

Miss Quimby, the dramatic critic of Leslie's Weekly and editor of its Women's Page, is the first woman to manipulate a monoplane. Two years ago she became interested in the flight of buzzards and she wrote an article suggesting that in order for the aeroplane to be successful, it must be devised in imitation of the buzzard's wing and tail. She has been making a careful study of aviation and is giving the results of her interesting experience in the air exclusively in Leslie's Weekly.[2]

In an August 5, 1909 article in *Leslie's Illustrated Weekly*, titled, "A Japanese Aeronaut to Startle the World" Harriet quoted a Japanese inventor as claiming that his "...study of the American buzzard and Japanese ingenuity would solve the perplexing problems of aeronautics."

It should be noted that Harriet's insight into the shape of a bird's wing and its relationship to stable flight was consistent with a minority of aviation "experts." The popular idea at the time was that an air machine needed at least two wings, that they be of a square design and they be held together with lots of glue and wires. The biplane design established by the Wright brothers was considered the design of preference. The minority view was that the single winged bird pointed to the monoplane design of the future. Quimby was among those believers.

In an subsequent article Quimby spelled out what she thought were prerequisites for a prospective student pilot. "One who has run a motor-

Fig. 2-3, Harriet Quimby, "The Dresden China Aviatrix"

cycle or an automobile successfully is all the better qualified to begin his lessons as an aviator. Without experience of this kind, the noise of the unmuffled motor in an aeroplane will be nerve-wracking."[3]

License Requirements

By today's standards, flight school in the early days was not very complicated. The first week was equivalent to today's ground school with the instruction devoted to daily lectures on the theory of flight and the basic construction of the airplane.

The second week the students did their "laboratory work," applying the theory learned the previous week. The students took apart and reassembled the various parts of the airplane and its motor. They were familiarizing themselves with the purpose and the mechanical linking between each part.

The third week was the student's first real exposure to a whole airplane. The technique was a distant cousin of the modern day simulator. The plane was similar to the one the student would eventually fly, but bolted to the hanger floor. This way the student could begin getting the "feel" of the engine and propeller under power. The rush of air was similar to what the student would experience in the air - yet the student could begin to manipulate the controls without any serious consequences.

The fourth week was the student's first exposure to an entire operating airplane. The craft, however, was not much of an aerodynamic specimen. It was heavy, well-built and designed not to get more than two or three feet off the ground. The important part of this phase of the schooling was learning to guide the machine in a straight line over a grass strip. Students showed promise if they drove anything that resembled a straight line on the first attempts. Quimby said, "This looks very easy until you discover that an aeroplane has the perversity common to all in-animate objects. It always wants to go the other way, instead of the straight way you seek to direct. Your first dash across the field and back takes two minutes, if no mishap occurs. After two dashes of this description, a discreet teacher will dismiss you for the day. You have had all that your nerves should be asked to stand."[4] If the student succeeded in driving a straight line six or seven times he (or she) then took short hops of two or three feet into the air as the plane rushed across the field. This maneuver was irreverently called "kangarooing" by a newspaperman. "It is not surprising," said Quimby, "that sometimes a fledgling student will forget what the instructor said about not moving the elevate lever and like a flash shoots the machine into the air. Finding himself much higher than he expected to go, he is likely to seek a sudden descent, involving both a breakage and humiliation." [5] "Breakage" as Harriet called it was a real problem with the rickety wooden planes. Each student paid $500 for the lessons, plus a $1,000 to $1,500 deposit to offset any damage to the airplane.

Once the student could steer the plane in a straight line, it was time to move into the fifth and an all-important week: the supervised solo. In a lighter airplane, the student made a series of supervised "jumps" of different lengths. A special device, fitted to the tail limited the altitude of the plane.

When the instructor felt the student was ready to fly, the student moved into the 30 horsepower Moisant-built monoplane. The aircraft was stronger than most of the aircraft of the day. The landing chassis was hickory, and the fuselage was spruce. The landing cradle was bamboo; and the highest grade piano wire was used to hold the wooden parts together. Imported French three-ply rubber-impregnated silk covered the wing and tail plane. The propeller was made of laminated mahogany or walnut.

Given the fragile construction of the airplanes, the temperamental nature of the engines, and the perfect weather conditions necessary for flight, Quimby's skill and her prelicense record speaks for itself. On one occasion, while attempting a takeoff, a wheel hit a gopher hole. The bicycle-like wheel separated from the undercarriage and the plane keeled over, breaking its wing. Quimby maintained her composure, shut off the engine and climbed out of the machine. She walked back to the take-off point, head held high, shoulders back and self-assured as if she had been out for a morning walk. That was the only mishap she had during her student days.

After Quimby mastered all the preliminaries, it was into the air. On her first sustained flight of several minutes, Harriet later said she felt "like a bird cleaving the air with outstretched wings."[6]

Since there was no windshield to protect Harriet from the direct propeller blast, when she landed her face around her goggles was covered

Fig. 2-4, Harriet Quimby ready for flight

with a mixture of fine dirt and oil. The Gnome rotary engine had a particular quirk that led to what some pilots called a "looseness in the lower gut." The engine, pilots said, was as clean as a pig in a mud wallow. Quimby remarked about the engine, "Not only is the chassis and all fixtures slippery with lubricating oil, but when the engine is speeded, a shower of this oil is thrown back directly into the driver's face. It is interesting that castor oil is the lubricant."[7] Most engines of the day used mineral oil, but in the rotary engine the oil and fuel mixed together in the hollow crank shaft. Vegetable-based oil did not break down when exposed to fuel, so castor oil was the substitute. The castor oil that did not burn went out the valves in a fine mist. The oily mist coated everything including the pilot, who could not help inhaling the warm gluey substance that resembled some of today's unhardened epoxies. See Fig. 2-4.

The Exam

It was July 31, 1911 when her instructor, Andre Houpert, gave Harriet the happy news. By late afternoon, the air was quiet, and after 33 lessons he felt Harriet was ready for her pilot's exam.

Quimby revealed in the August 24, 1911, issue of *Leslie's Weekly* in her article, "How I Earned My Aviator's License," that the actual time spent in each lesson was between two and five minutes and she had spent a total of less than two hours in the air. She pointed out that was the allotted time for students at each lesson taught in the leading French aeronautical schools. Her course of instructions covered many weeks due to adverse weather conditions. There were many days when the wind prevented even the most experienced pilots from going aloft. In the article, she attributed her success to a competent instructor, and the "kindly" hand that fate dealt her.

John Moisant had said that he believed no one could learn ". . . the thoroughness, the details of airplane construction, repair, adjustment and flight in less than five weeks and may take longer depending on the student's aptitude."[8] Albert kept to this schedule after John's death, and he held Harriet and Matilde to this standard.

The pilot's exam consisted of three parts: the first two parts included five alternate right and left turns around pylons, and completing five figure-eights. The third part was a landing test. Houpert had called two officials from the Aero Club of America - the licensing agency in the United States for the Federation Aeronautique Internationale - to witness the test. At first the Aero Club officials were skeptical about a woman flying, not believing that a woman could possibly pass the tests. They also resisted making the trip from New York City, but Houpert told them that another student, Ferdinand De Muria, was also hopeful of taking the test. Since a man would also be taking the examination, for the Aero Club license, the officials had no choice but to make the trip.

When the officials arrived the wind was calm. Houpert and the Aero Club officials decided to have Quimby run through the tests. Houpert had not told Harriet about the test, for he felt it would make her nervous. Although he had kept her in the dark about how much progress she was making he had a high degree of confidence in Harriet's ability, otherwise he would not have risked having her go through the tests. His reputation as an instructor was on the line too. Once Houpert informed her the Aero Club officials were there to review her performance she stepped up to the challenge with an air of confidence. She was annoyed that she had no prior notice but she also knew she could fly better that some of his other students and she was confident in her own ability. She knew this was her big chance and she would conquer the doubt held by the officials. This obstacle Harriet felt must be overcome, too. Harriet completed the first and second part of the test with ease. However, the landing test required her to land within 100 feet of where the plane had left the ground, and on her first attempt, she landed too far from the spot. The Aero Club officials were relieved that they did not have to grant Harriet Quimby her license. The wind was acting up so the officials agreed to stay overnight to test De Muria the next day.

"Sleep on what happened here today," Houpert said. It will give you some insight." That evening Quimby discussed her experience with her friend Matilde. "The test was not difficult," she said. "I just miscalculated the landing."

Matilde was encouraging and supportive, and encouraged Harriet to take the exam again the next day. "I encouraged Matilde to take the test also," said Harriet. "It would be nice to share our victories together." Matilde agreed to try for her license, but only after Harriet had completed her tests. Years later, Bobbi Trout, another aviation pioneer related to the author why Matilde Moisant took second billing. "She wanted Harriet to have the fame associated with being the first woman to earn her pilot's license. Harriet had declared to her friends that she intended to become a professional aviator, and Matilde knew that if Harriet was the first to earn her license it would enhance her image and her career." (At the time, Moisant herself had not yet thought about going into aviation as a profession.)

Harriet was in bed by eight-thirty, but she did not get much sleep, thinking about the landing test and what had gone wrong. She recalled in her mind's eye the entire test. Tomorrow, the results would be different.

Dawn
It was four-thirty in the morning. The light was just creeping over the horizon as the telephone rang in Quimby's room. It was the Garden City Hotel's wake-up call. The hotel was one of the most elegant on Long Island. Each room having a phone was a luxury only the best hotels in Manhattan could offer.

Harriet enjoyed fresh air, and weather permitting, always slept with the windows open. The birds were beginning to chirp and the air coming in the open window was heavy with the odor of the fields, trees and flowers. The birds had not yet begun their morning serenade. It was a time when nature seemed at rest, and Harriet felt the day seemed especially right for flying.

Quimby dressed quickly and met Matilde for breakfast. The clerk at the front desk waved to get Quimby's attention. There was a message from Houpert. He had telephoned the hotel and left a message advising Harriet the flying field was covered with fog. He had cautioned her not to come out until he called. There was no point waiting around for the fog to lift. Sometimes it remained cloudy or foggy all day. Harriet smiled when she read the message. Her friend had instinctively known that she would not be discouraged by the events of the previous day. He knew Harriet would not give up, and she would be back to try again. Soon after Houpert's call, while Harriet and Matilde were having breakfast, the judges from the Aero Club arrived in the dining room.

Quimby greeted them with excitement, and proclaimed that she was ready to retake the exam. The two men, however, tried to dampen her enthusiasm. The officials encouraged the women to ride with them out to the field in the surrey provided by the hotel. They said the fog might prevent anyone from taking the exam and patronized Quimby by saying that they hoped she would get a chance to show them if she could really fly. As they were about to leave for the field Matilde announced that she too would try for her license. The officials gave her a serious look, but said nothing except, "We'll see."

"They were not the least bit encouraging," Quimby remembered. "They were reserved, and polite, but verbally skeptical of our ability." That did not deter or intimidate Quimby. She knew she could pass the test. But she said, "It was a somber and stressful ride. The weather did not look promising either. The fog hung low to the ground and we drove through the thick, unheavenly mist. It seemed to grow thicker each foot we traveled, and the air was heavy with moisture."[9]

Many of the pilots of the day called the aerodrome on Nassau Boulevard the finest flying ground in the United States. It was just 20 miles from the heart of New York City, and the transportation facilities were "unexcelled both by auto and electric train."

When Quimby's party arrived at the field on the Hempstead Plains, the fog had reduced visibility to less than 50 feet. Quimby met Houpert with a questioning look. She could see that he was irritated that she had disregarded his instructions about waiting for his phone call. He shook his head and in his customary, laconic style said, "We must wait." See Fig. 2-5.

"We waited, and waited, and waited," said Quimby. "There was gloom within the hangar, and gloom outside. Our chief mechanic cheered us by predicting the fog would be gone within the hour. He was right. Soon the sun began to assert itself, and burn through the thick mist."

The activities of the instructor and students suddenly became a striking contrast to the lethargy of the preceding moments. Even the school mascot, a little dog named Spot for the black mark on his forehead, was alert and interested in the bustling activity.

The other students, all hopeful that one day they too would be ready for this day, paced the hangar, made small talk or quietly examined the monoplanes. Quimby had a worried look on her face as she looking at the little red flag at the end of a tall, skinny bamboo pole placed in the middle of the field. The fog had lifted, but the wind had also picked up. There was considerable misgiving as the light piece of bunting fluttered

Fig. 2-5, Harriet Quimby (r) & Matilde Moisant waiting with Andre Houpert for the right wind conditions.

from its mast. Harriet wondered if the wind would quiet down and she could get on with the test.

Houpert too wondered about the wind and settled the question by walking out on the open field with an anemometer. An anemometer is a hand-held instrument that resembles a windmill with cups instead of blades. It measures the breeze by the speed at which the cups revolve. Houpert was going to measure the velocity of the wind. If he returned and told the group the wind was over five miles an hour, the test would be off for the day. A student who ventured into anything more than a five mile per hour breeze - especially in a low powered monoplane was inviting serious trouble.

Several weeks earlier, Quimby described to the readers of her column another way of measuring the wind. "Only a year ago Glenn Curtiss gauged his air safety by cigar smoke. Not being a smoker, Mr. Curtiss would distribute several cigars noted for the heavy smoke they produced when lighted. A smoker would light one of these cigars and, holding his head back, blow the smoke straight into the air. If the smoke rose straight up, it was good flying weather." Quimby then described a recent "improvement" in technology. "Now one will often see an aviator pull a handkerchief from his pocket, and, holding it at arm's length in the air, judge the velocity of the wind by the fluttering of the linen."[10]

Houpert returned to the group without any emotion in his face. The group waited anxiously for a sign. He looked at Quimby, smiled and said, "It is time." Some of the students scurried toward the dressing rooms. They were going to cover their clothes with one-piece buttoned mechanic's suits of heavy coarse cotton, calculated to withstand wear and tear and oil stains. The other students dragged chairs out of the various dressing rooms and lined up near the takeoff point. They hoped that after Quimby, Houpert would then give the nod to Ferdinand De Muria, and Matilde Moisant.

The moment had arrived. Quimby climbed into the single seat craft. The crowd that had gathered the previous day, attracted from nearby Mineola and Garden City by the fast-spreading rumor that a woman was attempting to earn a pilot's license, was much larger today. The crowd was silent as the mechanic primed the engine by turning or "pulling through" the propeller. Two men held the tail, and another two crouched beneath the wing holding the landing gear. Harriet checked her controls. She had only a warping lever/control stick and rudder bars. The primitive craft lacked ailerons, so to raise and lower the wings Quimby had to twist the stick that, in turn, twisted the entire fragile wood and silk-covered wing. Quimby flipped a switch to engage the battery and raised her arm, the signal for the mechanic to give a strong swing to the wooden propeller. The igniter on the spark plugs glowed from the battery current and when the mechanic swung the propeller it allowed the fuel to come in contact with the glowing head of the spark plug. The 30 horsepower engine coughed to life, as the fuel ignited. The propeller spun blindly at 1,400 revolutions per minute (rpm). The engine's three cylinders spewed oil-filled smoke on the four men straining to hold back the aircraft. For a moment Quimby's face was hidden by the thick white smoke. When the smoke had dissipated, clearing her vision of the field in front of her, she raised her hand in a thumbs-up position. The men released the plane. It catapulted forward, bouncing down the rut and bump-filled grass strip for about 50 feet. On one bounce, it leaped upward. Quimby pulled back on the stick that operated the elevating surface on the tail. The craft was flying!

Quimby was about twenty feet off the ground, when an unpredictable gust of wind hit the monoplane from the left side. The right wing dropped dangerously close to the ground, and the crowd gasped, anticipating the worst. Quimby applied full opposite stick, to warp the wing and pulled back on the elevator control. Moments passed but slowly the right wing began to rise and the craft returned to the normal take off attitude. The crowd released a collective breath.

Quimby was at an altitude of about 150 feet, and all was going well. Her speed over the ground was about 45 miles per hour when she executed the first of her turns.

Turning in a Bleriot-styled monoplane required a high degree of dexterity and control. Quimby had to keep her eyes on the horizon, and she had to maintain the wings in an absolute level attitude during the turn. This required making only a very flat skidding turn, using the rudder. She had to coordinate the turn by keeping her eyes on the ground markers that indicated her turning points.

Again, the air acted up. A gust of wind blew the right wing up, lowering the left wing into a dangerous position. Quimby, unruffled, instinctively applied full forward pressure on the stick. She had to turn into the dropped wing to gain airspeed to pick up the wing. If she didn't do this, the plane could stall - and fall like a stone. It had happened before to luckless beginners. The craft was also nose-heavy, as were all Bleriot-styled monoplanes, and Quimby had to keep shifting hands on the stick to rest her tired arms. A thought occurred to Quimby. What if the engine quit? This had never happened to her but Quimby knew she must pitch the machine downward and glide to a landing. She could not dwell on that possibility. The sound of the engine and the fine oily mist told her that the three cylinders were firing properly.

Quimby looked down and thought about how clear the ruts in the road appeared. She thought too of the recent statement she had over-heard in her office. "The airplane will make the submarine easy to see beneath the water and therefore seriously interfere with it as a weapon of war." Quimby was skeptical.

Her thoughts did not linger on the airplane's potential in war. Right now she had a more important task in front of her. Harriet circled the field and landed, completing the second part of the test successfully. The engine, although air-cooled, ran very hot, and it was necessary for all pilots of airplanes using this particular engine to land periodically. While she waited for the engine to cool down, she strolled by the crowd. There was tension in the air today. She could feel it pressing in on her.

Soon it was time for the third part, the landing test. The previous day, she had landed and, in her excitement, shut down the engine too soon. (There were no foot brakes in those days.) This time Quimby planned her landing from the air. She mentally marked her touch-down spot, took aim at the white square, and began to increase her glide slope. Just six feet off the ground she pulled back on the elevate lever, flared, and the plane's wheels touched down perfectly. She counted off three seconds then flipped a switch that shorted out the spark plugs and shut down the engine. A silence suddenly fell over the area. All Harriet could hear was the creaking of the spruce framework on the monoplane as it bounced along the grass strip. The craft gradually slowed to a stop - just seven feet, nine inches from the mark. Quimby had set a record! And the crowd cheered her accomplishment. For Harriet, the sound was intoxicating.

Her Pilot's License

Harriet knew it had been a good flight. "After the flight," Quimby said, "I removed my goggles, then climbed out of my monoplane and nonchalantly walked over to the two official observers sitting on wooden chairs beside the flight line. I looked one of them in the eye and said, 'well I guess I get my license.'"

The man hesitated, looked at his partner and then at Quimby. "I guess you do," he said reluctantly.[11] On August 1, 1911, Harriet Quimby became the first American woman to earn her pilot's license. She was the thirty-seventh person and the second woman in the world to do so. Baroness de la Roche, of France, was the first woman in the world to earn her license. (Many people in those days did learn to fly but never bothered to get a license. For example, Blanche Scott had soloed on September 2, 1910 and went on to perform at air shows, but had never gotten around to applying for her license.)

In an ironic note, no one from her own paper covered the history making event. However, a New York *Times* reporter covering the story described Quimby with "her face covered with grease and dirt, and her blue eyes flashing happily."[12]

"The following day my pilot's license was forwarded to me. It was neatly bound in leather and looked very much like a gentlemen's pocketbook. It read as follows:"

Federation Aeronautique International, Aero Club of America:
The Above named club, recognized by the Federation Aeronautique International as a governing authority of the United States of America, certifies that Harriet Quimby, having fulfilled all the conditions required by the Federation Aeronautique International, is hereby licensed as an aviator.
The civil, naval and military authorities, including the police, are respectfully requested to aid and assist the holder of his certificate.[13]

(The above text written in French, German, Russian, Italian and Spanish, appeared on the opposite side.)

The officials were reluctant to acknowledge that a woman had successfully invaded the fraternity of flying. One newspaper wrote that the Aero Club officials ". . . were forced to make the award owing to the splendid flying done at Nassau Boulevard." The crowd had also wondered how high Quimby had flown. Her plane seemed to go higher that anyone had ever witnessed before. An examination of the barograph (an early version of the altimeter) in Quimby's plane revealed that she had also set a new altitude record for a student. The previous record, one that all students aimed for but usually did not reach was - 164 feet. Harriet's barograph? It showed 220 feet![14]

As a beaming Quimby walked through the crowd, she noted that the women were as awestruck as the men. When a group of women stepped forward to congratulate her, Harriet commented that, "Flying seemed much easier than voting." Harriet's quip was not lost on her audience. The Suffrage Movement would struggle another nine years to win women the right to vote. Fig. 2-6.

The Aero Club officials reluctantly agreed to allow Matilde Moisant a chance at testing for her license, but not before the man whom they had come out to test in the first place had taken his test. Ferdinand De Muria then took off in his Moisant-built monoplane and did his figure-eights satisfactorily. However, his landing was too "hot." He overran his mark, and crashed into the tail of the only other monoplane on the field, the plane that Harriet Quimby had used. Not only did Mr. De Muria fail the test and damage both aircraft, he also prevented Matilde from trying for her license that day.

Twelve days later, when her craft was repaired, Matilde Moisant passed her license exam. She became the second woman in America and the forty-fourth licensed pilot in the world. She also set a record for a student that to this day remains unbroken: Matilde Moisant spent a total of 32 minutes in the air before qualifying for her pilot's license!

Matilde was a maverick, and did unconventional things. This quickly led to an admonishment from the sheriff of Nassau County, Long Island. He had declared that anyone flying on Sunday would be arrested for violating the Sabbath. Male pilots objected, but obeyed the order. But Matilde continued flying. The sheriff decided he would curtail Moisant's activities by arresting her. The following Sunday, Moisant took off under

Aero Club of America
297 Madison Ave
New York, N.Y.

August 2d 1911

Miss Harriet Quimby, 225 Fifth Avenue, New York City

MADAM: We take pleasure in informing you that in a meeting of the Executive Committee held this afternoon, you were granted an aviation pilot's license of the Aero Club of America. This book is all made up and lacks only the signature of our acting president, which will be obtained tomorrow morning.

We find that the only other aviation pilot's license granted to a woman under the 1911 rules is that of Mme. Draincourt of France, who passed the tests in a Caudron biplane.

Should no mail advice to the contrary reach us within the next few days from Europe, you can accordingly consider yourself the only woman to have qualified under the new 1911 rules on a monoplane.

Regarding the landing made by you at the close of your first distance test on August 1st, we would say that accurate landing is not a record internationally recognized so that we do not know how this performance compares with the best made in Europe. We can state, however, that at this date, it is the most accurate landing made in America in a monoplane under official supervision.

The American record for accurate landings is 1 foot, 5 1/2 inches by Mr. Sopwith on his biplane. We do not officially make any distinction between types of aeroplanes in this record; we cannot see, however, how there can be any objection to your landing being referred to as an "American record for monoplanes" at this date, as this is what it is in fact.

Yours sincerely,

C.F. Campbell-Wood (signed)
Secretary

Fig. 2-6, A copy of the letter from the Aero Club

Fig. 2-7, Matilde Moisant (l) & Harriet Quimby

his nose, circling the field, taunting the sheriff and his men. The sheriff and his deputies followed her in cars, but the plane outdistanced the posse. Matilde landed at a distant field, and was gone when the sheriff arrived. Later that day, when Matilde returned to the field, the sheriff caught up to her. When he tried placing her under arrest, an angry crowd gathered, preventing him from taking her into custody. Later, a court decided that flying on Sunday was no more immoral than driving a car on that day. See Fig. 2-7.

Most of the pilots in the early days of aviation flew close to the ground, where they felt safe. On September 24, 1911, Matilde Moisant soared to the then dizzying height of 1,200 feet. (Wilbur Wright had only set a world's altitude record of 320 feet on November 8, 1908, in Le Mans, France.) Two weeks later, Moisant became the first woman awarded the Wanamaker Trophy (sponsored by Rodman Wanamaker, a millionaire industrialist, advisor to the New York City Police Department, and aviation enthusiast), for an altitude record reported to be 2,500 feet; a truly remarkable accomplishment in those days, given the instability of the aircraft.[15]

Newspapers followed Moisant's triumphs as closely and with the same sexism as they did Quimby's career. One described Moisant as ". . . small in stature, and frail looking." The reporter unsuccessfully attempted to redeem himself by saying she was a woman of ". . . determination and courage, and her dark flashing eyes indicated quickness and recklessness."[16]

Andre Houpert, the Chief Instructor of the Moisant Aviation School, had first objected to women in the school. Impressed by the flying and safety record of Harriet Quimby and Matilde Moisant, he said he believed a flying machine was safer in the hands of a woman than in a man's hands.

Both Quimby and Moisant were exceptional students. Each had received her license without a single accident in the air. The belligerent attitude of many men had a lot to do with their success. "We will not take chances," Moisant said. "We will show them that we can fly, and we will not break either the machine or our necks in doing it."[17]

Moisant was also a firm believer in the "lucky" number 13. She was born Friday, September 13th, 1887, and she was the second American woman to qualify for her pilot's license on the 13th day of August, 1911 (although her license reads the 17th). She always numbered her airplanes *13*. Harriet encouraged her friend to join her as a professional aviator. The thought appealed to Matilde. There was a lot of money to be made by a good pilot so keeping with her superstition around the number 13, Moisant also gave her first international exhibition on November 13, 1911, in Mexico City.[18] See Fig. 2-8.

Harriet Quimby, like most pilots, also had her superstitions. Her defense against the malevolent gremlins was a necklace and bracelet. She never flew without them and they show up in almost every photo of her. Later she added a little brass idol called Ganesha to her collection of amulets.[19]

Harriet Quimby had many vocal critics concerned about her "immodest dress" and once she began to appear in public, her original flying outfit pieced together from men's clothing was simply unacceptable. Her critics said she was corrupting the public's morals by wearing men's clothes. Quimby was not happy with the idea of wearing men's clothes either.

What to wear was a problem women aviators faced for many years but in the early years it was a major social issue. For centuries society severely restricted women's dress and fashions. Skirts dragged the floor and corsets contoured the female form into exaggerated hourglass shapes. Frills, ruffles, and lace also weighed down the costumes, and gave women the look of over-decorated dolls. Long flowing skirts had risen slightly in the first decade of the twentieth century, but only a few inches. A Massachusetts school department manual dictated that women, "Must not wear any dress more than two inches above the ankle.[20]

Wide hats were also in fashion for women in 1911, but they were impossible to wear in an open airplane. The hats were platforms piled high with artificial fruits and plunder from the animal kingdom. While ostriches suffered the embarrassment of missing tail feathers needed to decorate these platforms, actual wrens and thrushes also appeared in frozen death, with wings extended. The star victim of the fashion industry was the egret. This bird was easily caught while it tended its young. The egret became the most popular of the hat ornaments. Quimby also raised the alarm in a June 8, 1911 article in *Leslie's Weekly:*

THE EARLY BIRDS

[Incorporated in the District
of Columbia, not for profit]

APPLICATION FOR MEMBERSHIP

To the Membership Committee:

The Undersigned Pilot hereby makes application for membership in THE EARLY BIRDS and agrees that, if found eligible and worthy, he will conform to the usages, customs and rules of the organization. He further states that:

His nationality is *American* ~~He received naturalization papers~~

~~on~~ .... ~~at~~ ....
(Strike out portion not applicable.)

He was born on *Sept. 13th* .... at. *Earl Park — Ind —*

His present occupation is ... *none*

~~He is connected with~~ .... ~~in the capacity of~~

His work in aeronautics began *July 13th 1911* .... at. *Long Island — New York*

He first soloed on *July 13th 1911* .... at. *Moisant School of Aviation*

in a. *Moisant Monoplane* .... and holds

Aero Club of *America* .... Certificate No. *44*

and he continued as follows:
(Give chronicle of experience and achievements.)

Learned to fly alone from the very first time I sat in the plane, in 32 minutes. An official record in Aero Club of A.

Further references to experience and achievements may be found in the following publications or records:
(References to magazines, periodicals, newspapers, papers, etc., with dates, are of interest.)

In submitting this application, the undersigned certifies as to its accuracy and truthfulness and that he has personally signed his full name thereto.

Date. *Oct 18th — 1935* .... *Matilde Moisant*
(Signature.)

Residence. *2538 Olive Rd — La Crescenta — California*

Business address ... *none*
(Print out.)

WE, the undersigned members of THE EARLY BIRDS, vouch for the good character and eligibility of the applicant and recommend his admission.

Proposer ... *D. B. Morrow*

Seconder ... *Ernest Jones*

Should it be inconvenient for the applicant to secure two members to sign this application, he may furnish three references who can vouch for him.

Name................................Address................................

Name................................Address................................

Name................................Address................................

Membership dues must accompany this application blank.   Dues enclosed $....*5.00*

(Extract from By-Laws.)
CHAPTER V. MEMBERSHIP AND DUES.

SECTION 1.   Membership shall be limited to those who piloted a glider, airplane, gas balloon, or airship prior to December 17, 1916, upon evidence deemed sufficient by the Membership Committee and approved by the Board of Governors, except that
Nationals of countries other than the United States engaged in the World War must have met the foregoing conditions prior to August 4, 1914.
SECTION 2.   Membership shall be as follows:
(a) Patron membership.
(b) Membership.
Patron membership may be secured by a member paying annual dues of Fifty ($50.00) Dollars or more.
Membership may be secured by a member paying annual dues of Five ($5.00) Dollars.
In all respects patron members and members shall enjoy the same rights and privileges of membership.

Fig. 2-8, Matilde Moisant's application to the Early Birds

I am trying to do my part in sounding a general alarm, and sending messages to about eighty million apathetic and easy-going people before it is too late. The time to send in a fire alarm is before your house is entirely consumed, and not after. For forty years, we have been smarting under the national disgrace of the wicked slaughter of the American Bison. If something is not done, and done quickly, we will be smarting under the disgrace of having looked calmly on while our American birds are slaughtered and gradually annihilated.[21]

Quimby urged her readers (at the time *Leslie's Weekly* had a circulation of over 325,000) to write to their senators and congressmen. The government eventually did hear the pleas of concerned people like Harriet Quimby and passed laws to stop the plunder. By this time, it was too late for the flamingo, passenger pigeon and great auk which had already disappeared from the United States.

But the issue of what a woman pilot should wear could not be resolved by an article in the newspaper. Pants - or trousers - and a man's shirt were the most practical form of clothing for pilots. For most American women emerging from the Victorian era, however, these were unacceptable or immodest. Some women attempted compromise, and wore trousers with rows of buttons on the inside that converted the garment to a skirt when not flying; others "hobbled" their skirts by tieing them below the knees. Women found this uncomfortable, awkward, and dangerous. Eventually, as other modes of dress became popular, a flying outfit would evolve for women pilots. It would, however, take years to gain public acceptance. The modest attire was a two-piece outfit, a blouse and wide-legged tweed knickers or riding pants with high-top boots and a soft fabric helmet with goggles.

Until that flying outfit evolved, Harriet Quimby and other women who dared to fly received definite signals from the establishment on what was inappropriate dress, and what roles women were to assume. Even her own newspaper took a position favoring the status quo. *Leslie's Weekly* ran an editorial on October 5, 1911, commenting on a sermon delivered by Bishop Nilan, in Hartford, Connecticut:

The bishop was particularly critical, and justly so, of the vulgarity of the costumes worn by women today. The 'master of fashions,' said he, seems to be preparing women to take their place with man by shaping her garments so that they often closely resemble man's attire, with the result that she disfigures her beauty and deforms her nature. Gone is the old-time womanly expression of sweetness and modesty, and in its place we have its swagger and stare. In the prevailing style of dress, women, without question are exposing their figures as never before in the history of civilization. Had the change come about all at once, it would have shocked the sex into a revulsion of feeling; but coming gradually, it has taken advantage of the weakness of woman to accept the style as handed down with too little protest. Through a little independence in their dress and that of their daughters, mothers of refinement may yet save the day for modesty and even virtue.[22]

Quimby approached her critics and this challenge with an air of dignity, flamboyance, and style. "It may seem remarkable," she said, "but when I began to fly I could not find a regular aviator's suit of any description in the great city of New York, and I tried hard. In my perplexity, it occurred to me that the president of the American Tailor's Association, Alexander Green, might be a good advisor; and he was, for it did not take him long to design a suit which no doubt will establish the aviation costume for women in this country, if not the world, since the French women continue to wear the clumsy and uncomfortable harem skirt as a flying costume." The outfit was extraordinary for 1911; a one-piece purple satin outfit with full knickers reaching below the knee, and high laced black kid boots. Her head gear resembled a monk's hood, and her accessories were flying goggles, elbow-length matching gauntlet-style driving gloves, and a long leather coat for cold weather flying. In colder weather, she wore a full length cape to match the purple outfit. The hood had small swatches of black net inserted over the parts that covered her ears, so she could "keep in touch" with the workings of the engine. "It was also an ingenious combination," she said. "It can be almost immediately converted into a conventional-appearing walking skirt when not used in the Knickerbocker form."[23] See Fig. 2-9.

Reporters were curious, and asked her why a beautiful and success-ful female journalist would instead of getting married and raising a family, want more from life. "I took up flying," Quimby told reporters, "because I thought I'd like the sensation. I haven't regretted it. I like motoring but after seeing monoplanes in the air, I could not resist the challenge. The airlanes have neither speed laws or traffic policemen, and one need not go all the way around Central Park to get across to Times Square. Then, too, it's good to be the first American woman to earn a pilot's license."

Quimby, perhaps more clearly than most people of her time - including her fellow aeronauts - saw the potential aviation had as an industry, and as a future source of employment for women. "I see no reason the aeroplane should not open a fruitful occupation for women. I see no reason they cannot realize handsome incomes by carrying passengers between adjacent towns, from parcel delivery, taking photographs or conducting schools of flying."[24]

There were those who were so vigorous in their opposition to women flying that they refused to sell a flying machine to a woman. Quimby used her Moisant-school connection, and soon had a 50 horsepower Moisant-built model of the Bleriot monoplane. Now she was ready to show America that women can fly as well as the men.

At first, reporters thought Quimby must be a radical feminist who was trying to raise America's consciousness about equal suffrage. Reporters asked her if she supported the suffragist's actions. She said no, but the reporters pressed her and suggested she name her craft for one of their leaders like, "Pankhurst" for example or "Catt." (Mrs. Emmeline Pankhurst, an English feminist, came to America in 1906, with her special techniques to heighten public awareness. Heckling meetings, mutilating art, and burning buildings were her ways of promoting the cause. Carrie Chapman Catt was an American feminist.) Harriet did name her flying machine but chose instead to call her new plane *Genevieve,* in honor of the patron saint of French pilots.

The flying machine was a spectacular phenomenon in 1911, and there were two major areas of debate in aviation: the safety of flying, and whether women should be flying at all. New and truly amazing records were being set with these fragile machines, but often would-be record seekers became part of a growing number of fatal statistics. There was a growing controversy about how much air safety was being compromised by these daredevils in the sky.

Men continued to kill themselves in the poorly designed and unstable airplanes. One pilot, Harry Atwood, had just set a long-distance record by flying 1,265 miles in 28 hours, 31 minutes, averaging a speed of 46 miles per hour. (Atwood, unlike most of his contemporaries died in his sleep at the age of 85.) All the positive publicity this record created was lost to events of the Great International Aviation Meet in Chicago that followed. The aviation meet did not start off well, with in-fighting and bickering over commissions to the pilots. Two fatalities further blemished aviation's reputation. Quimby, in her article, entitled, "The Dangers of Flying and How to Avoid Them," spelled out the problem. Simply put, it was male ego.

The Great International Aviation Meet which just closed at Chicago, teaches one vital lesson. The aviator should be thinking more of his safety and less of public acclaim. It also teaches promoters of meets to have greater regard for the lives of the flyers than startling the public with perilous exhibitions of stunts.

The sad and shocking death of two popular aviators and the great number of narrow escapes that took place day after day, involving a breakage of machines that will cost their owners thousands of dollars to repair, seems to justify the statement that the safety of the flying grounds, and of the flyers, was the last consideration of those in charge.[25]

This Meet was the first sporting event of its kind held in America. The flying was to be purely competitive with the absence of exhibition or guaranteed purses.

Harriet Quimby had gotten a letter from one of the flyers at the Meet. "You should consider yourself mighty lucky that the Chicago Committee did not come up with your price to come here to fly. Without exception the grounds are the worst I have ever seen for a tournament . . . a number of machines were damaged yesterday because of conditions."[26]

At the time there was a deeply rooted belief among pilots that when called upon to fly they must do so despite their judgement about the plane or conditions of safety. "The one great fear of the flyer," said

Fig. 2-9, Harriet in her famous flying suit

Quimby, "is that he may gain a reputation for being what is known as a 'ground hog,' one who has lost his nerve."

One newspaper report said that $250,000 had been raised for the event and yet the aviators who participated found this amount cut into prizes of one thousand dollars or less. "Most flyers risked their lives, and sometimes damaged their machines," said Quimby, "for a compensation that would scarcely cover their expenses. For a sportsman-like event, calculated to promote the science of aviation, this seems to me to be singularly unsportsman-like.

"For those really interested in aerial navigation for the benefit of mankind, the dangerous 'spiraling down,' and 'banking' not only lack entertainment, but are downright foolhardy. When this fancy flying has been cried down, the dangers of the air will be appreciably less."

In Quimby's day - and even today - most people acknowledge that every new invention has to go through its own break-in experience. Some people would not ride the first steamboat, because they were sure the boiler would explode. Some bitterly opposed the construction of the first railroad, because they said it would be deadly to run the train at full speed. Some farmers said it would be impossible to keep cows off the tracks. Despite these objections, steamships plied the oceans through storms in less than five days, and railroads traveled sixty miles per hour in Quimby's day.

"Is aviation dangerous?" Quimby asked in her article. "Yes, so is swimming," she said, "if one tries to swim through Niagara. So is skating on ice that is thin. Bicycling, motoring and many other activities in which we constantly indulge are perilous unless conditions are made comparatively safe. Over good ground, flying on a calm day, driving an aeroplane is as safe as driving an automobile in a crowded city. Over a ground filled with holes and ruts which send up gusty whirlpools and cause treacherous 'air pockets' aeroplanes become hazardous. Yet with a clear-headed pilot, it need not necessarily be dangerous."

Quimby also talked about the "wonderful improvements" in airplane technology. "The invention of the biplane, which is simply a box kite properly balanced and equipped with steering planes and a motor has done much toward progress in air navigation. But the biplane is not like a bird nor does it fly like a bird. Everyone who has seen the monoplane with its long and narrow body and its outstretched wings will agree. The monoplane is a real bird of human creation. What the monoplane has done to promote the science of flying is being proved everyday by men making one thousand mile flights without a mishap. The craft of today is in an imperfect state. But the great number of fatalities are not due to the imperfections of the machines. In nearly every investigated case, the fatality was shown to be reckless flying."[27]

Harriet made her point by listing nine fatal airplane accidents, seven of which were in biplanes.

Quimby was also correct in assessing reckless flying as a major cause of fatalities but the machines also shared some of the blame. Cal Rogers began an attempt at a transcontinental flight on September 18, 1911. His flight lasted 49 days and after dozens of crash landings, a few broken bones, and hundreds of repairs to his aircraft, he landed in California, on November 5. While he was the first person to fly successfully across the country, his flight emphasized the dangers, lack of scientific knowledge about flight, weather and the poorly constructed craft. His flight in the fragile "Vin Fiz" was an adventure in danger and daring. Like many of his contemporary aeronauts, Rogers did not live long enough to enjoy his fame. He died a few weeks later - in an air crash.

Flying Pays Off

Soon after receiving her license, Quimby earned her first professional fee: $1,500. For most pilots in those days, earning money was difficult. A pilot needed a license to appear at professional meets, and unless the pilot owned the machine, it was often a hand-to-mouth existence. A flyer could usually negotiate between 20 and 35 percent of the net earnings of the meet. From this, however, the pilot had to pay for mechanics, transportation of the craft on a train to each meet, hangar fees, fuel and other sundries like tips to all the tag-alongs who followed, waiting to minister to the pilot in a awkward form of hero worship. A pilot was ahead of the game if his net earnings was ten percent over his expenses. The lion's share of the profits always went to the manufacturer or suppliers of the machines.

Harriet set her first official record at her first air meet. On September 4, 1911, with a crowd of 20,000 persons gathered at the Richmond

County Fair (at Dongan Hills, on Staten Island at the site of what today is the Berry public housing project), she became the first woman to make a night flight.[28] The crowd was so enthusiastic over her appearance that Quimby had to help officials clear the landing field of people before her flight could begin. Quimby jumped in her red Roadster and helped clear a path for her takeoff.[29]

The moon was full and the air was calm when Harriet took off across the Narrows of New York Bay, the busy shipping channel for the Port of New York. She climbed to about 2,000 feet and then returned to Staten Island. As she approached the field, the playful side of her character emerged. Like a falcon, she swooped down over the judges and the grandstand. She and the crowd got such a thrill out of this, she did it again. As she flew over, Quimby waved her white handkerchief. The crowd went wild with applause. Even she could hear the applause over the roar of the engine.

As Quimby made her approach for a landing, the crowd surged out of the stands and onto the field. Unknown to them, this jeopardized her landing and made it dangerous. She flew over the heads of the crowd, and dropped down sharply just beyond them. The craft bounced several times into the air, nearly throwing Quimby out of the seat. It came to rest just a few feet from the boundary fence. The only damage was a few broken wires.

When Harriet dismounted the machine, her mother rushed up to her daughter, hugged her and kissed her repeatedly and then admonished her. "You were up there almost seven minutes," she said, "and I think I would have come up after you had you not come down when you did." Quimby answered, "Oh, don't worry, mother, you'll get used to it. It was grand. I did not feel like ever coming to earth again."[30]

After the flight, reporters asked Miss Quimby about the feeling of flight. She replied, "It was a great temptation not to keep right on flying until I got to New York. The funny thing about it was I was so hot up there. I think it was the effect of the applause that made my blood rise. I never heard so much applause before."[31]

The press goaded Quimby from time to time. On one occasion, they asked her why she limited her flights to short hops. The Bleriot-style monoplanes, and her Moisant-built monoplane, were some of the most difficult machines to control at the time. Designers of the machines had not yet solved the unstable characteristics common to monoplanes of the day. Beginners like Harriet worked up to long flights by taking short hops to become more acquainted with the machine's particular characteristics. Quimby replied confidently to the reporters, "I have not found it very difficult to control my monoplane in short flights, and there is no reason I soon shouldn't make longer ones." Soon Quimby was making longer trips.

Repeated rebuffs did not have a discouraging effect on Quimby either. She persisted in overcoming negative attitudes, and found other ways to accomplish her goals. Quimby was asserting her rights - and those of all women.

Once she insisted on her rights Harriet encouraged other women to do the same. She overcame man-made obstacles on the ground, and in the air she handled her machine with the skill of the best of the male pilots. Quimby was quickly gathering loyal admirers, both male and female.

Her advocacy of women's rights attracted the few men who also believed that women's potential was still an untapped resource. Harriet received anonymous poetry from shy men, and dozens of written marriage proposals. In addition she received gifts in the mail and at every flying event where she appeared. The gifts were mostly personal and ranged from flowers to jewelry, but included a few household items too. Harriet Quimby was becoming America's sweetheart. The flowers she appreciated and enjoyed; the gifts she returned whenever possible, with a warm note of appreciation, but with a firm request not to repeat the kindness. She did not want to be seen accepting gifts from perfect strangers, that would certainly cast a shadow on her character. Her many admirers sometimes made it difficult to focus on her flying career and maintain her independence. She would not, however, compromise her goal of becoming America's most famous aviator.

Quimby did not have trouble finding work or an income from her flying. During an air meet in September, 1911 at the same field on which she had learned to fly, the Nassau Boulevard airfield, Harriet Quimby beat France's leading woman pilot, Helene Dutrieu, in a cross country race and won the purse of $600. Just two weeks later, she flew a demonstration flight at the Trenton State Fair in New Jersey, and earned another $1,500.

As Quimby's fame began to spread some exaggerated and untrue stories surfaced. One magazine ran a story that she was "the daughter of the Wild West," an accomplished bronco-busting cowgirl. Another said she had driven her Roadster alone as far as Kansas City.

Matilde Moisant also had her share of excitement. Not long after Moisant earned her license, she had the first of several brushes with death. On September 10, 1911, Moisant was descending through a cloud and fog bank, back to the airfield. When she broke into clear air, she found herself on a collision course with another plane. She quickly made a sharp right bank and narrowly missed the other machine. The radical maneuver caused the monoplane to stall and begin to fall out of control. Only her skill saved the plane and her life. She recovered the plane from the plunge, and landed to tumultuous applause.[32]

Off To Mexico

In October, 1911 Harriet Quimby could be found writing an aviation article in her stateroom on the liner *Lampasa*, on her way to Mexico. Matilde Moisant and the other members of the Moisant International Aviators Exhibition Team were going on a flying tour of Mexico. The team's six monoplanes, and two biplanes - plus the mechanics - were on their way by rail. The two biplanes, purchased from the United States, were the first ever sold to Latin America.

The group had been invited and guaranteed a $100,000 purse to participate in the inauguration ceremonies of President Francisco Madero. Matilde Moisant was the first person to land a plane in Mexico City. The troupe started in October and toured the country through December. The Mexican people seemed even more in love with Harriet than her American fans. Most people in Mexico had never seen an airplane much less one driven by a beautiful woman.

Quimby's day-to-day experiences gave her fodder for her pen. On one flight, she lived a pilot's nightmare. Her engine failed. Harriet remained cool-headed and remembered the three rules her instructor had taught her. Dive the craft at a slight angle to gain air speed and control, look for flat ground, and land quickly. The third rule, Houpert had told her was inevitable, but if the event should ever occur, he said she must do it with style and grace, but if that was not possible, just do it. He also told her the speed and control at which she executed this maneuver was critical. Too steep an angle and she would gather too much speed and perhaps go out of control. Control he said was critical. Harriet maneuvered the plane to a slight diving angle, feeling the plane wanting to go steeper, she manipulated the elevate lever until the craft was gliding safely toward a wide open field. She was able to land safely in the field - but not before exercising excellent judgement and gliding over and barely missing several trees. Quimby proceeded to write an article on how to fly safely. As random chance would have it, the same type of incident befell Matilde Moisant, in Guadalajara. Matilde did not have an open field in which to land and crashed. The plane flipped over, crumbling around her and pinning her in the wreckage. Fortunately a guy wire prevented the engine from crushing her, and she escaped serious injury.

The team had planned on spending the winter in Mexico, but political unrest and the rebel Emilio Zapata caused a sudden change in plans. The Moisant aviation team literally flew from the jaws of danger when the rebels attacked the *Federales* in the town in which they were giving an exhibition. Mexico had become too volatile - so the group went back to the United States.

By this time, Quimby's fame was spreading like a prairie fire. The editor at *Leslie's Weekly* saw the sales potential and encouraged her new-found second career. He asked her to write about her adventures in Mexico and flying in general. Every issue that carried an aviation article by Quimby was sold out.

Some months after Matilde earned her license, her friend Harriet Quimby began to notice a subtle change in Matilde's attitude about flying. "I believe it was her anxiety over John's death that led her to become less conscientious about her flying. As a result, Matilde had three serious accidents. That of course, would dampen anyone's enthusiasm."

Matilde Moisant Retires from Flying

After Mexico, Matilde and Harriet parted company for awhile. Moisant continued to fly with Moisant International Aviation, touring the South, but Harriet had other plans.

Although Moisant and Quimby both had exceptional skills, the frequency of flying these unstable machines increased the odds of having an accident. Moisant had a series of accidents that several times reduced her machine to a pile of firewood, and ultimately ended her flying career.

Matilde Moisant narrowly escaped death at Shreveport, Louisiana, when the plane descended too sharply, bounced into the air, and turned over. Again, only a guy wire prevented the machine from crushing her.

Despite these hair-raising escapes, it was only after much persuasion by Andre Houpert, her former instructor, that she decided to retire. Moisant picked Tuesday, March 12 1912, to announce she would make her last flight the following day on March 13th, her "lucky 13," in Kansas, Texas. Andre Houpert, and some of her friends suggested she quit while she was ahead but she said, "I wanted the sensation of a farewell appearance." It turned out to be nearly the last thing she ever did.

"I mounted my machine, circled for about ten minutes and attempted to descend. Then the crowd rushed toward my machine. I knew I had to kill someone or take a chance on myself. I chose the latter. My machine shot up about thirty feet, and came down with such force that the gas tank came loose. Instantly the machine was on fire. Mr. Houpert, my former instructor had anticipated trouble and quickly rushed to my rescue."[33]

A cowboy friend of hers also anticipated trouble with the crowd and was galloping toward where she was going to land, in an attempt at holding back the crowd. Houpert and her ground crew, risking their lives, dragged Moisant from the burning machine. Her clothes were on fire, and Moisant had also been burned around the face. The rescuers threw extra coats and blankets around her to squash the flames. "In five minutes," Moisant said, "the entire machine had been destroyed and the crowd was swarming around its skeleton. That was my last flight." Moisant's first words after being pulled from the fiery jaws of death were to notify her sister in a nearby hotel that she was safe. Moisant owed her escape to the heavy tweed knickers, coat, thick leather helmet, and high-laced boots she was wearing. True to her word, she gave up flying, but hinted that she may come back to fly for amusement. "I have the air intoxication," she said, "and only a flyer knows what this means.[34] I could never watch my brother flying without experiencing great fear within me. But after I leave the ground I enjoy every minute without a thought of anything that might happen." She paused and in her eyes tears welled up. It was a painful memory. "The earth is bound to get us after awhile," she said. "So I shall give up flying before I follow my brother." See Fig. 2-10.

After Houpert had witnessed Moisant narrowly escape death he reversed his earlier position on women flying. Moisant - and other women - he said, were better suited for almost any other occupation.

When World War I broke out, Matilde Moisant - like many women pilots - volunteered to go overseas with Pershing's expeditionary force, as a pilot. The government's reply to her request was polite and protective. "It is not the intention of the United States to take women into the actual dangers of the war zone unless the need becomes imperative."[35] (It would be more than 60 years before the U.S. military would seriously consider allowing women pilots in the armed forces, and almost 20 years after that, before they seriously addressed the issue of women pilots in combat.) After being repeatedly rejected, Moisant became a Red Cross nurse and served in France until the end of the war.

What To Call A Woman Pilot?

By 1912, Harriet Quimby was one of the most skilled pilots of the day and the highest profile female flyer in America. But some people still doubted her ability - even after she proved she could fly. Quimby's response to these critics was, "There is no more risk in an airplane than in a high speed automobile, and a great deal more fun to drive. More American women drive cars than English or French women, and yet there are already several French women aviators. Why shouldn't we have some good women air pilots, too?"[36]

Another problem arose as women began taking to the sky. People wondered what to call Quimby and other women pilots. Some editors used the word *aviatrix*, and others *airwoman*. Still another said why discriminate? Why not lump all pilots under one term, aeronauts?

Fig. 2-10 Matilde Moisant's plane on fire

The New York *Times* said, "The difficulties to be overcome in establishing a permanent glossary of terms for this rapidly developing science of aeronautics seem formidable." The *Times* finally reported that the neutral term *aviator* was acceptable for both sexes. America, however, was not ready for a non-gender related term, and *aviatrix* remained in use for many years. In fact it still was showing up in the 1990s.

"Once I had my license," said Quimby, "I realized I could share the thrills of aviation with my readers. I wrote in the first person because they would feel closer to the events in the cockpit." Quimby also wrote a thrilling account of her English Channel crossing, "An American Girl's Daring Exploit." Harriet was showing American women that there were alternatives that would give them new adventurous directions in which to chart their futures.

The First Cross-Channel Airwoman.
From the London Sketch.

Fig. 2-11, A London newspaper story of Harriet Quimby's victorious Channel crossing

Miss Harriet Quimby, an American, 25 years old, had been staying at Dover, England, as "Miss Craig." She left Dover early one morning not long since and, flying in a Bleriot monoplane, passed over Deal and across the Channel, landing at Hardelot, near Boulogne-sur-Mer. Thus she made the first flight across the Channel by a woman alone. The daring airwoman's costume was of navy blue satin. It consisted of knickers, bodice and hood all in one piece. Her flight began at 5:39 a. m. from the aerodome, three miles outside Dover. She was at a height of 1,500 feet above sea-level when she left England and at a height of 2,000 when she reached France. She was one hour and nine minutes making the crossing.

Chapter Three

Flying the Channel

"I was annoyed from the start by the attitude of doubt on the part of the spectators that I would never really make the flight. They knew I had never used the machine before, and probably thought I would find some excuse at the last moment to back out of the flight. This attitude made me more determined than ever to succeed." - Harriet Quimby, 1911

Harriet Quimby was determined to show women they could branch out and try new experiences. The idea that had been born during her Mexican tour was about to become a reality. It had quietly grown in her mind during the long and cold winter in New York. Harriet decided that she would be the first woman to fly across the English Channel. Preparations for this adventure had to be made in secret. If someone found out, they might try the flight first. She made plans to travel to England, telling people she was going to try her luck in contests with French women aviators. When she sailed for England on March 7, 1912 on the liner *Amerika,* less than a dozen people knew her real plans. *Leslie's Illustrated Weekly* quietly agreed to sponsor her flight and she traveled with her business manager and friend, A. Leo Stevens, the balloon designer and pilot. Stevens was an old hand in the fledgling world of aviation. He owned a balloon "foundry" which produced spherical balloons on order, and he also held Aero Club license Number 2, as a balloon pilot. Later he became one of the first civilian inspectors of aircraft for the U.S.

Fig. 3-1, Louis Bleriot's monoplane

Army. Harriet also carried a letter of introduction to the noted European airplane designer, Louis Bleriot.

When Quimby arrived in England, she and Stevens approached the London *Daily Mirror.* As a journalist she suspected that the *Mirror* might agree to an exclusive story in exchange for a European sponsorship. The *Mirror* officials were shocked that a woman would attempt such a dangerous flight, alone. But they also recognized that Quimby was an American, someone from the "Colonies" as they put it. The British also knew that stranger things happened in America. After Quimby and Stevens spent the better part of the afternoon discussing the advantages the *Mirror* would gain over an exclusive story, the paper agreed to the sponsorship. They would back her efforts with, as Quimby put it, "a handsome inducement" of $5,000 for exclusive European publication rights to her flight. (*Leslie's Illustrated Weekly* had exclusive U.S. rights.)

Quimby and Stevens then sailed across the English Channel to meet Louis Bleriot, in Calais, France and inquire about buying an aircraft for the flight. "I never was the best kind of sailor, and there was a real satisfaction in contemplating the crossing in the air and mocking at the waves that had so often made me uncomfortable."[1]

Louis Bleriot had recently introduced a 70 horsepower monoplane. It was fast and maneuverable, and Quimby wanted to use it for her Channel crossing, and then take it back to the United States. Bleriot informed her that although in production, the plane would not be ready for at least two weeks. Quimby knew each day that passed made it more likely someone else would attempt the crossing. After long and difficult negotiations, Quimby proposed to buy a new Bleriot 70 horsepower monoplane - if Louis Bleriot would lend her a 50 horsepower model for the Channel crossing while the other plane was finished. Bleriot reluctantly agreed to the terms. Fig. 3-1.

The danger of the flight was clear to Quimby, Stevens and Bleriot. Louis Bleriot was one of the few men who had succeeded in flying the Channel. He was taking a chance on losing one of his airplanes if Harriet did not succeed in the flight. But he had heard of Harriet's skill as a flyer. He also had a deposit on the new plane and a promissory note signed by Stevens to pay for the plane in the event it was lost. It was strictly business for all concerned. The two men had a lot riding on Harriet's skill and courage. Stevens knew Harriet and was confident in her skill. He believed in her and was willing to risk the investment. Bleriot was covered either way fate dealt the hand.

Bleriot's hanger was at Hardelot, where he had a seaside home. Harriet had never flown a true Bleriot type monoplane and she said, "It seemed prudent to try out the machine first in some quiet way. So Mr. Bleriot shipped it to Hardelot. I followed soon after. According to Mr. Bleriot, the control of the new machine was different from that which I had been used to in the United States, hence my desire to have a trial flight." Actually, the 50 hp Bleriot was a different plane from a power, design, and handling point of view, from the Moisant-built monoplane Quimby had been flying.

Quimby described the little French town where she intended to make her test flight. "It was not easy finding Hardelot. It was a summer resort of recent creation, and its elusive character, as well as its remoteness from the crowded cities, made it a good place to test my machine without attracting attention. There was a fine hotel at Hardelot I was told, with several handsome cottages and some all-year round homes including one occupied by the Duke of Argyle. The route from Paris to Hardelot is via Boulogne. When I reached Boulogne, I could not find a cab or other conveyance to carry me to Hardelot. I finally found a ramshackled tramcar. It was the Easter holiday, the tram was crowded, and all I could get was a place to stand. As people got off, they tripped over my luggage which was pushed all over the floor of the tram," she said. "They were not happy climbing over my luggage and showed it in their looks. I was not happy either in the way they treated my luggage, or me!"[2]

After a trip that took well over two hours, Quimby finally arrived in Hardelot. "To my chagrin," said Quimby, "the fine hotel I had heard of was closed and dark. I then found out that the hotel opened only in the summer time. I had a dilemma. I had only a fragmentary knowledge of the language and I was among strangers. I did have good fortune, however. I found a small cottage that accepted lodgers. Between my limited French and their halting English I was able to communicate my situation. They were able to give me a night's lodging and a simple but tasty meal." Harriet was not used to the accommodations that greeted her in this quiet rural French town. "My room was very tiny and chilly without a carpet. It had a single frame bed, a feather-filled comforter, for which I was later grateful as the chilly night air swept over me, and a washbasin.

"I had scarcely sat down to eat when a small girl, the owner's daughter, asked me to sign a card. It seemed someone in Calais had been talking about my impending trip and the little girl wanted my autograph. My question - can a man keep a secret? I was now concerned that they knew of my plans in England."[3]

Grounded By Bad Weather

The weather in France also did not cooperate with Quimby. It turned horrible. "I was eager to test the machine and rose early the next morning. To my extreme disappointment I found the wind blowing like a gale. We waited all day long, hoping it would quiet down, but instead it kept increasing. It whistled around the corners of the building at a velocity of 40 miles per hour. The next morning the wind had not let up and I had to sit in that cheerless room and wait."[4]

Quimby did not despair. She remained positive, knowing things would work out. Once again good fortune smiled upon her. "An English family, living in Hardelot, heard of a lone American, a stranger in a strange land, and sent an automobile and an invitation to lunch with them. I gratefully accepted and remembered their kindness later."[5]

Quimby could not wait any longer for the weather to clear to try her new Bleriot monoplane. She was anxious to get back to England where she was sure word had leaked out about her up-coming record-making trip. "Before I left Calais on Saturday, April 13, I took an automobile three miles out from the city to inspect the spot from where Mr. Bleriot started to make the first successful aeroplane flight across the Channel on July 25, 1909. A fine granite monument marked the spot where he flew from Calais to Dover. It seemed to me that the Dover Cliffs were higher, and I preferred to make the flight in reverse of Bleriot's direction."[6] Quimby would make her flight in the same direction as her mentor John Moisant. The first American to fly the Channel, in 1909, Moisant made the trip three times and an overeager reporter erroneously stated that on one trip he took his favorite pet, a cat named Miss Paris.

In the three years since Louis Bleriot had made the flight, the development of the airplane had fostered the talk of a regular airplane passenger service from Dover to Calais. Considering the actual state of aeronautical science, the talk was optimistic and premature by years.

The Bleriot monoplane was a frail, spindly-looking machine. Louis Bleriot was the son of a successful fabric manufacturer, but he became a wealthy man in his own right. He financed his experiments in aviation by the invention of a successful automobile headlight. Bleriot also had a stunning series of failures before his successful Channel flight in 1909. He had manufactured eight different models ranging from cellular wing gliders to canard aircraft. Most of them either crashed, burned, or scattered themselves across the vineyards of southern France. Until his 1909 model came along, Bleriot was infamous for surviving all the accidents in his errant aircraft. Bleriot flew all his designs and developed a technique that may have saved his life on several occasions. When he was certain he was going to crash, he would roll the airplane on one wing and use the wing to cushion his impact.

The Bleriot, although a primitive design by today's standards, was significant in the evolution of aeronautical development. Even today airplanes can trace their roots to the Bleriot design. Louis Bleriot created the enclosed fuselage, the engine placed forward of the pilot, the single tractor propeller, and the rudder and elevator placed on the stabilizer on the rear section of the fuselage. He even built a partially swiveling landing gear trying to compensate for a crosswind landing.

The 1909 Bleriot and the rear-elevator Curtiss aircraft were the two most widely copied airplanes of their day. (John Moisant, only working from photographs of the early Bleriot designs, was one of the successful copiers.) The Bleriot design was light and simple to maintain, as well as easy to disassemble and set up for flight. From the perspective of the early exhibition pilots this was an important benefit. The Bleriot could be assembled and ready for flight in 30 minutes, while the Curtiss or other biplane designs took six to eight hours to assemble. Another factor that gained the Bleriot its popularity was the air-cooled Gnome Rotary engine it used. This engine gave the Bleriot an extraordinary edge because of its reliability (over the liquid-cooled engines) and its low weight per horsepower. The Gnome engine was only about 580 pounds, compared to the 985 pound engines of the biplanes.

The Bleriot was also literally a wood and canvas airplane, held together with wire and glue. The fuselage alignment, wheels, tires, tail surfaces, and flying wires all had to be examined before each flight. Any wire not properly attached and secured had the strength of a child's kite string. The wing warping device and the strange shaped wing were also invitations to trouble. If the flying wires around the warping device were tightened too much, an over-eager pilot could very well apply too much warp to the wings and snap the wire. The alternative to this was an overreaction that caused the wire to tear the wing from the plane. Clearly it required an alert, resourceful professional to successfully handle the craft.

After several days of fruitless waiting for the weather to clear, it was evident to Quimby that she was wasting valuable time. She must get back to England. She had arranged for the airplane to be shipped in secret to an airfield in Dover, on the coast of England. When she arrived back in England, Quimby registered under the name "Miss Craig" to avoid being recognized, if word had leaked out. She knew how reporters could be and the story of her proposed flight would make front page news and possibly encourage others to try and beat her to the goal. No sooner had she registered she learned that at another woman had flown across the Channel. Just days before, Eleanor Trehawke-Davis flew as a passenger in a plane flown by Gustav Hamel, a pilot who had successfully completed the trip three times. Davis was not a pilot, but an aviation enthusiast who admired Quimby. She owned two Bleriot monoplanes and had hired Hamel.

It bothered Quimby that someone on the *Mirror* had leaked the story, but she was more annoyed that they had withdrawn their "handsome inducement." They also dropped their exclusive coverage of Quimby's story, since Davis made the flight. This setback, Harriet decided, would not discourage her spirit. She could still be the first woman to pilot a plane across the channel. Men had been making the trip for almost three years, it was time for a woman to pilot a plane across the Channel. While there were women flying in Europe at the time, none had dared to challenge the dangerous Channel flight. Quimby believed being the first woman to pilot a plane across the Channel was a bigger and more lasting prize than Mrs. Davis' fleeting publicity as a passenger, and the prize was hers if she acted quickly.

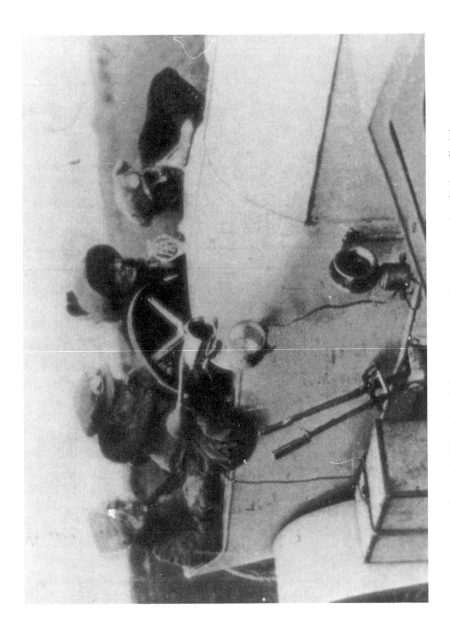

Fig. 3-2, Harriet & her party on the way to the flying field

Quimby still wanted a few practice flights in the new airplane, but the weather over England and the Channel would not cooperate. It was worse than the weather she had left behind in France.

Clear Weather

Dawn on Sunday, April 14, 1912, brought a near-miracle. The weather had cleared virtually overnight. Quimby and her eager party drove to the Aerodrome three miles outside Dover to look at the newly assembled monoplane. See Fig. 3-2. The controls looked the same as her Moisant-built monoplane, and she wondered about its control. Harriet had learned to fly in a 30 horsepower Moisant-built plane, and flew the 50 horsepower model in air shows. But this plane was genuine 50 horsepower Bleriot, and Louis Bleriot and Gustav Hamel both said it would be more difficult to handle.

The weather was perfect - the air was clear, and Harriet could just make out Calais, dimly outlined 22 miles across the Channel. There was no wind and the sun was bright in the aqua blue sky. Those present - including the reporters - urged her to take off immediately, make a practice flight and then take off for Calais to take advantage of the clear weather. The forecast for the following day was for high winds and rain that may last for days. Previous experience with flights from the Dover aerodrome had shown that absolutely still air was necessary. To their disappointment, Harriet refused to fly. It was Sunday, the Sabbath, and she had promised her mother she would not fly on that one day for any reason. Her ground crew and curious onlookers soon began to leave. Soon Harriet was alone with Stevens. He was not puzzled by her refusal to fly on such a perfect day, and knew her well enough that he would not waste his breath trying to change her mind. They drove back to the hotel talking eagerly about her flight the next day.

The primitive weather forecast of the previous day was correct. Monday brought thick clouds, dangerous gusting winds and heavy rain over Dover and the English Channel. "I was not nervous about what lay ahead of me, I was impatient to get going, despite the protests of my friends," Quimby recalled. "I was going to fly on the other side of the Atlantic for the first time. My anxiety was not getting started quickly."[7] Harriet and her small ground crew sat all day in a damp hangar at the aerodrome, waiting for the weather to clear. The reporters also waited, but slowly they left, convinced not even a crazy person would fly in wind and rain.

Hamel knew the dangers of such a trip and knew too that there was a vast difference between crossing the Channel as a passenger with an experienced pilot and making the crossing alone for the first time. As they sat in the hangar, Hamel made an offer to Quimby. "On the eve of my Channel crossing," said Quimby. "Mr. Hamel was convinced that a woman could not make the trip alone. He was so anxious for my safety but I think also secretly that he questioned my ability to pilot the airplane across the Channel, he suggested dressing up in my flying costume, flying across the Channel and landing at a remote spot where I would be waiting to take the credit. I adamantly refused his offer, and would have been very angry if he were not such a valuable technical consultant. Mr. Hamel offered to show me how to read a compass and I did accept this offer. That was something new to me. I was annoyed from the start by the attitude of doubt on the part of the spectators that I would never really make the flight. They knew I had never used the machine before, and probably thought I would find some excuse at the last moment to back out of the flight. This attitude made me more determined than ever to succeed."[8]

Takeoff

"All things come to those who wait," thought Quimby. On Tuesday, April 16, 1912, the rain had stopped, but there was still patchy fog in the area. "At three-thirty Tuesday morning we were called, had our hot tea and biscuits, got into our automobiles and at four o'clock were on the flying grounds. It was chilly, but there was no wind, and scarcely a breath of air. We pushed the monoplane out of the hanger and waited for the first light of day. We knew we must hurry, for it was almost certain that the wind would rise again, soon after sunrise." See Fig. 3-3. Hamel was still feeling some guilt over being an accomplice on Mrs. Davis' trip, and volunteered to test fly the Bleriot monoplane after the assembled airplane was checked. "I shall always remember Mr. Hamel's courtesy," said Harriet. "He jumped into the machine and was off for a short try-out of the engine and report the atmospheric conditions. Hamel hurried back and made one of the beautiful and easy landings he was famous." The machine checked out perfectly. "Now it was my turn," said Quimby. The

Fig. 3-3, The courageous Harriet preparing for her flight

sky immediately over the aerodrome was clear, but the French coast, unlike two days ago, was totally obscured by a moving wall of mist. Harriet decided it was time to make history. See Fig. 3-4, 3-5.

Quimby took off at 5:30 a.m.. "I could see people waving handkerchiefs but the engine roaring at 1,200 revolutions per minute drowned out what surely were cheers and wishes for my safe journey."[9] See Fig. 3-6.

Later Quimby reflected, "On takeoff, I saw at once that I had only to rise in my machine, fix my eyes upon Dover Castle, fly over it and speed directly across to the French coast. It seemed so easy, like a cross-country flight. I am glad I thought so and felt so, otherwise I might have had more hesitation about flying in the fog with an untried compass, in a new untried machine knowing that the treacherous North Sea stood ready to receive me if I drifted off my course. This was the fate of D. Leslie Allen, the English aviator, who started the same day as I did, in a monoplane similar to mine, on a flight over the Irish Channel, from London to Dublin. He started, but he never came back. It is a mystery of the Irish Channel.

"I started climbing steadily in a long circle, and soon reached an altitude of 1,500 feet. As I looked down, Dover Castle was in a veil of mist. I could barely see the tugboat filled with reporters sent out by the *Mirror* to follow my course. The fog quickly surrounded me like a cold, wet, gray blanket.

"The tugboat trailed a long stream of black smoke, and the boatload of reporters whom I suspected were also would-be rescuers tried to keep up with me, but I quickly out-distanced them. They disappeared completely as I climbed and the fog thickened. I think they thought I was trying the machine in a test flight, and they must have been astonished when the monoplane gradually melted into the mist and the engine sound faded."[10]

Hamel had only given Quimby brief instruction in reading a compass. She had never seen one operating in a moving plane. "I had never used a compass, and I was doubtful of my ability to read one. Mr. Hamel said it would be shaking from the engine vibration, and difficult to read. I was hardly out of sight of the cheering crowd before I hit a heavy fog bank, and found the compass to be of invaluable help." Quimby had only two instruments with her: She wore a watch on her wrist, and held the

Fig. 3-4, Harriet putting on her heavy gloves

compass between her knees. "I could not see above, below, or ahead. I started climbing to gain altitude, hoping to escape the fog. It was bitter cold, the kind that chills to the bone. I climbed to a height of 6,000 feet looking for a hole to escape the mist that engulfed me."

Under her flying suit of wool-backed satin, Quimby wore two pairs of silk combinations, and over it a long woolen coat, an American raincoat, and around her shoulders a long wide stole of sealskin. Even this did not satisfy her solicitous friends. At the last minute, they handed her a large hot water bag, which Hamel insisted on tying to her waist.

"I soon found I was not too warm. The Channel passage was chilly enough, especially when I shot through the damp banks of mist that speedily enveloped me. But I did not suffer from cold while crossing. The excitement, I guess, stimulated me. I noticed when I landed the hot water bag was ice cold. I'm sure it helped, but I didn't notice."

Quimby also wore Scotch woolen gloves that gave her good protection from the cold, but the machine was wet from mist and her face was covered with dampness. "I had to push my goggles up to my forehead. I could not see through them. I was traveling at a mile a minute and the mist felt like tiny needles on my skin," she said.[11]

During the flight, Harriet recalled Hamel's remark about the North Sea. If she drifted off course by as little as five miles, she would get lost and probably go down in the icy waters. (Hamel should have taken his own advice as seriously as he had given it to Quimby. Later he flew off into the Channel mist, and never returned.) Harriet also recalled the Frenchman, Jean Blanchard who a century before had made the trip in a balloon leaving his fate to the fickle winds.

Danger Over the Channel

Quimby followed the compass needle faithfully. It was her only frame of reference and reassurance. Around the mid-channel point, the fog was beginning to take its toll on her nerves. Her head ached from the strain of keeping the craft level. Her senses were keenly aware of the attitude of the plane. The concentration on the task was exhausting. The minutes ticked by like hours as she listened to the sound of the engine. If the engine should quit, she realistically knew she had little chance of surviving a crash-landing in the cold, fog-shrouded waters of the Channel. She decided to descend and look for clear air. As she lost altitude,

Fig. 3-5, Hamel making sure Harriet is secure in her seat.

Fig. 3-6, Harriet's ground crew hold back the monoplane while Harriet listens to the sound of the engine.

Fig. 3-7, Harriet is writing a telegram advising her friends in Calais that she is safe.

the machine tilted to a steep angle, causing the gasoline to flood the engine. This was a design flaw that already had proven fatal for several pilots. The machine began to backfire. Quimby regained control of the craft and began to consider her options. She had but one choice, she thought. "I figured on pancaking down to strike the water with the plane in a floating position. (The plane had a balloon-like floatation device running the length of the skeletal frame. It is doubtful however, that it could have kept the airplane a float for very long.) "To my great relief, the gasoline quickly burned away and my engine began an even purr. I glanced at my watch and estimated I should be close to the French coast."[12] Soon the little Bleriot broke through the mist and into the brilliant sunlight. A gleaming strip of white sand, flanked by green grass, caught Quimby's eye. The fog had disappeared and she knew she was safe. Because of strong crosswinds and the underpowered 50 horsepower engine, the 22-mile trip took one hour and nine minutes.

Success

Harriet recalled seeing landfall. "Meanwhile the wind had risen and the currents were coming in billowy gusts. I flew a short distance inland to locate myself or find a good place on which to land the machine. I was happy to be ashore but I could not find Calais. The land below me was all tilled and rather than tear up the farmer's fields I decided to drop to the hard sandy beach. I did so at once, making an easy landing."[13]

Quimby jumped from her machine and found herself alone on the shore. But the solitude, the sudden silence that surrounded her after she shut down the engine, lasted only for a few minutes. A crowd of fishermen, women, and children all carrying pails of sand worms came rushing from all directions toward her. "They were chatting in French," she said, "and I understood enough to discover that they knew I had crossed the Channel. These humble fisherfolk knew the significance of what had happened. They were congratulating themselves that the first woman to pilot an airplane across the Channel had landed on their fishing beach."[14]

Harriet Quimby landed her Bleriot just two miles from the small village of Hardelot, the same village she had gone to borrow the Bleriot. The monoplane had returned like a homing pigeon to its nest. "It was nearly seven o'clock and I felt like eating breakfast. I knew my friends at

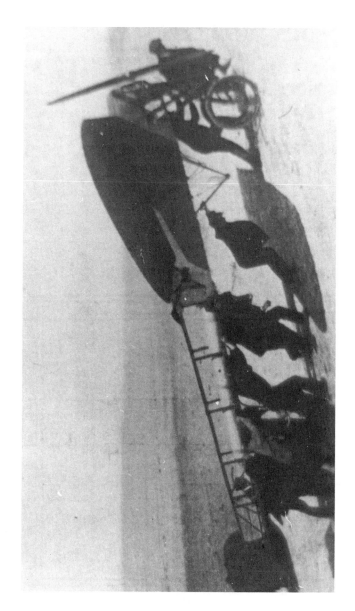

Fig. 3-8 The fishermen dragging Harriet's craft to safety

Fig. 3-9, Harriet Quimby enjoying her tea on the French beach.

Dover and Calais were anxious to hear the results of my trip. Just before I had started, someone had thrust a London *Mirror* between my woolen coat and my raincoat, as a further protection from the cold. I tore off the margin of this paper, sat down on the sand and wrote a telegram, while the curious fishermen looked on. See Fig. 3-7. From one of them, I learned that Hardelot was the nearest place and about two miles. I asked a fisherboy to take the message for me. I had no money to pay him as I had expected to land at Calais, where friends would be waiting. But the fisherboy took the message and the operator sent it. Who paid for it I do not know. Then I hunted up a life saving station nearby, and one of the men kindly telephoned to Boulogne the news of my safe arrival. This was also without charge.

"I had to send these messages by someone, for I feared leaving my airplane with an inquisitive crowd of strangers who had never seen one at close range before. Perhaps I had misjudged the fishermen. They were helpful and thoughtful in every way. Taking note of the rising tide, they made me understand that the airplane should be moved higher up on the beach. An airplane is difficult to handle. I did not want my machine harmed so I picked out an elderly, sensible looking fisherman who seemed interested in the mechanism, and put him in charge of the moving. It was pleasant to notice the gentle care these fishermen and even the children gave to handling the airplane." The good-natured people of the small fishing village were thrilled that a new heroine had literally dropped in on them. They were ready to do anything for Harriet. They were only too willing to pull her machine over two miles through the sand, and put it back into the Bleriot hanger in Hardelot. See Fig. 3-8.

"An incident that pleased me more," said Quimby, "was the hospitality of one of the fisherwomen. She insisted on serving me a very welcome cup of hot tea, accompanied by bread and cheese. She served me the tea in a cup fully six times as large as an ordinary teacup and it was so old and quaint that I could not help conceal my admiration of it. The good-hearted woman insisted on giving it to me, and no cup that I have ever won or ever shall win as an aero trophy will be prized more than this cup." See Fig. 3-9.[15]

It was not long before all the people of Hardelot were racing to welcome the fearless air traveler. "Among the crowds arriving on the

Fig. 3-10, Harriet Quimby victorious!

beach," said Quimby, "I recognized my good English friends with whom I had lunched just days before. They were so glad to see me safely across the Channel that they impulsively lifted me upon their shoulders and carried me over the sands. I felt more uncomfortable at that moment, than I had during the trip. Perhaps I should not admit it but I note the fact because the *Mirror* photographers and moving picture men, who on hearing of my landing had rushed over in their automobiles from Calais. They caught this scene with their cameras, and that means they will give it to the public."[16] See Fig. 3-10.

The newspaper reporters arrived and produced a bottle of champagne from a place of careful concealment. It was barely past 7:30 a.m., but they insisted that Quimby permit them to drink to her health while she sat on the machine. "Of course I did," she said, "anything to oblige these faithful recorders of the day's events. But the real refreshment I confess was that cup of hot, fragrant tea."[17]

Harriet's dream had come true. She had finally achieved her goal. She could almost see the headlines around the world. "America's Daring Premier Female Pilot Conquers English Channel." In a tragic and ironic twist of fate, the world's newspapers did not carry headlines proclaiming Quimby's historic flight. The headlines focused on a tragedy that eclipsed all other world events. On April 14, in the darkness of the North Atlantic, the "unsinkable" White Star liner *Titanic* struck an iceberg and plunged more than two miles into the black abyss beneath the waves. The sinking of the *Titanic* on its maiden voyage, with more than 1,573 lives lost, was the most shocking sea disaster the world had ever seen. The *S.S. Carpathia* had barely reached the survivors, and had not yet assessed the situation when Quimby launched her monoplane off the white cliffs of Dover toward France. When Quimby landed on that Normandy beach, word of the tragedy had not yet reached the sleepy village of Hardelot. The jubilant French farmers turned her into an instant hero and had a party in her honor that lasted until the late evening even though Harriet had been driven back to Calais in time to catch a fast train back to Paris. She arrived in Paris at 7 p.m., "a very tired but very happy woman."[18]

Quimby then sailed back to England, and booked passage back to America. There would be no welcome or parade for Harriet in England. A tragedy impossible for the human mind to comprehend just 24 hours earlier now weighed heavily on everyone.

The trip across the Atlantic back to America was filled with anxiety for everyone aboard the *Amerika*. There was a memorial aboard the ship, on the first day out of England. If the unsinkable *Titanic* had gone down so quickly, with so many souls aboard, what chance did those on a smaller ship really have? To add to the general anxiety, storms swept the Atlantic, lashing at the ship throughout the voyage. Despite the general depression among the passengers on the ocean liner, Quimby remained upbeat and positive. She dined with the ship's captain, had passengers toast her victory, and autographed photographs taken by the ship's photographer. She had accomplished her goal - and no one could take her victory away. But in the quiet of her stateroom, Quimby could not help but feel sorrow and offer a prayer for the souls who had gone down to the sea in the *Titanic*. This tragedy, she knew, would be long remembered. Her victory - well, she was not sure it would be remembered at all.

Sour Grapes

The wireless telegraph had flashed the news of both Quimby's victory and the *Titanic's* tragedy across the ocean. Even before Quimby had left England the *New York Times* wrote a biting comment of Quimby's feat. The editorial, dated April 18, 1912 and no doubt influenced by the paper's opposition to the suffrage movement that was in full flower in the spring of 1912 said, "Exultation Is Not in Order. Even when so much public attention is on the loss of the *Titanic,* the fact that a woman alone, depending wholly on her own strength, skill, and courage, has driven an aeroplane across the English Channel, does not pass unnoticed.

"Miss Quimby's flight is a considerable achievement. Just a few months ago this same flight was one of the most daring and in every way remarkable deeds accomplished by man. Since then the passage has been repeated by men, and now for them there is little or no glory. The flight is now hardly anything more than proof of ordinary professional competency."

The *Times* continued its condescending warning stating, "The feminists should be somewhat cautious about exulting over Miss Quimby's exploit. They should not call it a great achievement, lest by so doing they invite the dreadful humiliating qualification, great for a woman.

"A thing done first is one thing done for the seventh or eighth time is different. Of course it still proves ability and capacity, but it does not prove equality."[19]

The smell of these sour grapes still lingered by the time Harriet's steamship arrived back in New York on May 12. She received no hero's welcome, and there was no ticker-tape parade. It was a matter of timing. Only a week earlier, 15,000 women and about 600 brave men marched up Fifth Avenue in support of women's suffrage. The male leaders of the city had not yet recovered from this demonstration of feminine assertiveness and they were not ready to admit there existed female eagles, let alone honor them. Ironically, the suffragists also gave Harriet the cold shoulder; to them the only thing worse than an anti-suffragist was an independent woman uninterested in their cause.

Quimby was not a woman who would let an anonymous editor have the last word. "I wish I could express my views on this," she wrote. "It's not a fad, and I did not want to be the first American woman to fly just to make myself conspicuous. I just want to be first, that's all, and I am honestly delighted. I have written so much about other people, you can't imagine how much I enjoy sitting back and reading about myself for once. I think that's excusable in me."[20]

Eight decades later it may be difficult to understand the danger in the 22-mile Channel flight. But put Harriet Quimby's accomplishment in proper perspective: only nine years had gone by since the Wright brothers' first powered flight in a heavier-than-air machine. Bleriot's monoplane had a reputation as the trickiest aircraft the French designer had yet produced (although his next design would be worse). Several flyers attempting the flight had been lost and by all the 1912 rules of flying, Quimby should have turned back. Those rules were simple: One did not fly in the fog, rain or clouds, at night, or in more than a five mile per hour wind. There were no parachutes in those days, no guidance equipment, radio or navigating charts. A flight over water, out of sight of land, was perilous. For Quimby, this was the first over-water flight, fog and rain obscured most of her trip, and it was her first blind flight using a compass. In addition, she flew a plane that warped its wings to bank, and its engine needed equal amounts of gasoline, prayer, and luck. Her airplane, simply put, was scarcely more than a winged skeleton with an underpowered motor and no instruments, and a craft with which she was unfamiliar. Surely, to fly across the 22-mile English Channel, in 1912, required extraordinary courage, skill, and self-confidence. She had to keep the Bleriot on an even keel, with no horizon as a frame of reference. Quimby, however, played down her feat. "The trip was as easy as sitting at home in an arm chair," she said, "and I never had any doubt of my success." On another occasion she said, "Any woman with sufficient self-confidence and a cool head could fly across the Channel as easily as I did. Within months, probably weeks some other woman probably will make the same flight or even achieve some greater undertaking."[21]

Quimby also recognized and discussed a topic that for years after her death would be cited as a reason women should not fly. "Driving an aeroplane is more a matter of personality than sex, since it requires so little physical strength. There is no sport that affords the same amount of excitement and enjoyment in return for so little strength. It is easier than walking, driving an automobile, easier than golf or tennis.

"Men flyers have given the impression that aeroplaning is very perilous work, something an ordinary mortal should not dream of attempting but when I saw how easy men flyers handle their machines I said I could fly. Flying is a fine, dignified sport for women, it is healthy, and stimulates the mind."[22]

Quimby then tweaked an exposed nerve. "I believe women are more fearless than men, or at least I have more requests for rides from them. Many women write to inquire into the possibilities of aeroplaning as a sport, or as an occupation. It is the present high cost of the machines that prevents many women from flying. I believe that as soon as the price of a machine is within the range of the average person, flying will become a popular pastime for women."

Quimby's remarks was a sage commentary on the future. A main drawback to women throughout the history of aviation was and still is economics. For the first fifty years of women's involvement in aviation, society held rigid rules. If a woman worked, she often worked longer hours for less money than her male contemporary. So for women to be active in aviation, she often needed to be financially independent. This economic disadvantage only began to get wide spread attention beginning in the 1960s with the modern feminist movement. The economic factors and the affordability of flight lessons are still major restrictions to more women becoming involved in aviation today.

Chapter 4

The Boston Air Meet

"There is nothing to fear if one is careful. Only a cautious person should fly. I never mount my machine until I check every wire and screw. I have never had an accident in the air. It may be luck, but it is also to the care of a good mechanic." - Harriet Quimby, 1912

Quimby's aerial adventures were building her a solid reputation as a skilled aviator, but there was no substantive action to encourage other women to fly. She was a lone voice in the wilderness, mostly ignored by the male-dominated system. Her articles on the developing science of aviation had raised the awareness of the possibilities for women to fly, but she was the only writer encouraging women. She was also extremely sensitive to the possibility of negative press and its effects on furthering women's acceptance in aviation. A manufacturer had offered to teach women to fly if they then worked as demonstration and test pilots, but Quimby did not think this was a good idea. She knew the ever-present dangers of flying a tested machine and felt that the manufacturer's offer was clearly taking advantage of women and in the long run would add to the negative image of women pilots. In her *Leslie's Illustrated Weekly* column she wrote, "The offer is dangerous and foolhardy. Testing new aeroplanes does not seem to me to be exactly the right kind of work for a woman. But, I see no reason she can't if she chooses. The manufacturers

Fig. 4-1, Blanche Scott pictured in 1912

are saying that if a woman could fly their aeroplanes then the craft and flight itself must be safe. A skilled flyer would be a good advertisement for a manufacturer but a very dangerous proposition for a man or a beginner. The remuneration for a demonstration flyer is far more than for a mere flyer. Some men flyers in Europe try this work, but only a few very good flyers succeed at it."[1]

There was a Long Island flying school that offered a 10 percent premium to anyone who got through the course without any "breakage." The school was running little risk in its offer since, as Quimby wrote, "The history of aviation to this point has not seen a case of extreme good luck."[2] The school where Quimby had earned her license required $500 for the course and she needed an additional $1,500 deposit for the test.[3]

Harriet was already a successful journalist but she wanted a good income to support herself and her parents. She had decided that she wanted to be financially independent. Harriet also had dreamed of becoming a successful fiction writer. As in all fields then - and many still today - Quimby did not earn the equivalent of the male journalists. Quimby would surely earn more money writing fiction. At the time, only about 25 percent of the female population in the United States worked outside the home, and they earned on average less than $5 a week, less than half of what men earned.[4]

By 1912, social changes in the status of women were becoming obvious. When Quimby had begun her career as a journalist, there were not many women in the field even though a woman, Elizabeth Mallet, started the first daily newspaper in the world, *The Daily Courant*, in England, in 1702. More women had successfully integrated journalism and some were seeking admission to the prestigious schools that led to higher paying jobs. These attempts to gain admission to the top schools of journalism, had generated strong and vocal opposition from many men in the field. They perceived the economic threat the women posed. James M. Lee, Director of the NYU School of Journalism published a rebuttal to the opponents of admitting women to the Pulitzer School of Journalism at Columbia University. His comments were appropriate for women in journalism and for women in aviation as well. "The question," he said, "is not whether women should go into journalism, they are already in the profession, but whether they will get an honest deal at the school. Even if states object to giving votes to women, it does not necessarily follow that we should object to giving notes on journalism to women. The public and the publication alike are not so much interested in the sex of the writer as they are in securing the best work whether by man or woman. Give women a chance."[5]

Quimby had found the means to reaching her goal of financial independence was through the growing popularity of air meets. The Boston Air Meet attracted the biggest names in aviation. Headlines blared, "Come See America's Greats - Daredevil, Lincoln Beachy; "Nerveless" Charlie Hamilton; and the "Queen of the Channel Crossing - Harriet Quimby."

Other women pilots like Blanche Scott had registered in the event, but Quimby was undoubtedly the main attraction. See Fig. 4-1, 4-2. Harriet was in an exhilarated mood on Monday, July 1, 1912, the second day of the meet. She was at the peak of her career, and receiving acclaim wherever she went. Everyone loved her. She was billed as "America's First Lady of the Air," and after this performance she would be very close to her goal. She could retire from flying and write fiction, although she knew in her heart of hearts she would never completely retire from the air.

Top Event

The event featured many well-known aviators: Lincoln Beachey, Glenn Martin, and Earl Ovington were among the top names. The promoters of the air meet, held at Harvard Field on Squantum Bay, had money on their minds. So did Quimby's manager, A. Leo Stevens. He had a unique package to sell, and he drove a hard bargain. Quimby was the world's best known female aviator, and this was her first public appearance since her victorious Channel crossing. She also was flying her new and more powerful Bleriot monoplane. Quimby's trusted friend, Matilde Moisant, described another reason Stevens was a tough negotiator. "Harriet was the prettiest girl I have ever seen. She had the most beautiful blue eyes - oh what eyes she had. She was a tall and willowy brunette, and when she wore her long cape over her satin plum-colored flying suit, she was a real head-turner." See Fig. 4-3, 4-4. William Willard, the meet's manager, agreed that Quimby was an irresistible drawing card, and reluctantly conceded to Stevens' terms, $100,000 for Quimby's

Fig. 4-2, Harriet posing next to her Bleriot monoplane.

seven-day performance. Other top-billed male aviators also attempted - unsuccessfully - to negotiate what were outrageous sums in those days.

Quimby was proud of her flying record. The fragile airplanes of the day would sometimes break up in flight and failure of the unreliable engines had caused many accidents and fatalities. The Bleriot had a wing-warping device that in the hands of a pilot who overreacted could literally twist the wings off the plane. Quimby never had a flying accident because she was a careful and capable pilot. She gave close attention to every wire and fastener before each flight. "I had confidence in my craft," she said. She had written an article for *Good Housekeeping* entitled "Aviation As A Feminine Sport." Its aim was to give women confidence in their ability to equal the performance of men. "There is nothing to fear if one is careful," she said. "Only a cautious person should fly. I never mount my machine until I check every wire and screw. I have never had an accident in the air. It may be luck, but it is also to the care of a good mechanic."[6]

It was early evening, and time for Quimby to fly her last routine of the day. She had challenged the record of the English pilot Claude Graham-White who set an overwater speed record of 58 miles per hour, a year before. Quimby was going to break his record. Again she was going to fly an unfamiliar plane. She had brought the new machine back with her from France, and, after the boat docked and Quimby had cleared Customs, the inspector asked to see her again. No one knew how to classify her Bleriot monoplane, so they sent her to the legal department. After a long discussion, the lawyers told her that the Customs official had put a number on the form that suggested a polo pony, and since he did not have a category for an airplane, he did not have a problem with the classification. The lawyer went on to say that under present law, the airplane as a vehicle did not exist in their books. Customs officials and the lawyers discussed the problem for over an hour. Some wanted to call it a phantom horse and pretend they did not see it come ashore. They resolved the problem by putting it under the category reserved for polo ponies with the footnote, "One flying machine - equivalent to 70 horses."[7]

The new high-powered, two-passenger machine was originally designed for military use. It was fast, and could climb easily - but it was also difficult to control. It was, many agreed, the trickiest aircraft the French designer had yet to produce. The balance of the airplane was

Fig. 4-3, Harriet Quimby in her famous satin flying outfit.

critical. With no passenger in the rear seat, a sand bag provided artificial ballast. The gyroscopic effect of the big Gnome engine with cylinders revolving around the drive shaft was also known to cause control problems. It took all of Harriet's skill and experience to successfully fly this Gallic beast. She had made three practice flights in the new plane in late June, and one earlier on the day of the speed challenge. She was developing a good sense of how to handle the machine. During the second practice flight, Harriet substituted a passenger, Walter Bonner of Montana, for the sand bag ballast, and became the first woman to fly a passenger in an aircraft.[8] On her return trip to the Mineola landing field, Quimby encountered Cecil Paoli, who at the time was the youngest licensed pilot. The eighteen-year old Paoli lined his airplane up in race fashion and Quimby took on the challenger. They flew neck-in-neck back to the field, with Quimby pulling out ahead in the final minutes of the flight. She crossed the imaginary finish line (the beginning of the field) a full plane-length ahead of Paoli.[9]

On Quimby's third practice flight, again with sandbag ballast, she was climbing to altitude when the machine shot up in the air, dipped its wing. The craft stalled and began to fall uncontrollably. The plane dipped its nose to a steep angle, but Harriet had the presence of mind to neutralize the controls, and the Bleriot recovered from the spin, Harriet regained control of the machine and landed without further incident. She mentioned this unusual behavior of her machine to her mechanic Mr. Hardy when she landed. An inspection of the machine did not reveal anything out of the ordinary. Hardy could not explain the incident and said that sometimes airplanes lose their balance in the air, especially when hit with a gust of wind.

Tragedy

William P. Willard, the manager of the Boston Air Meet, and his pilot son, Charles, tossed a coin for the honor of flying with one of the Meet's most famous pilots. William Willard won the toss, and headed for the Bleriot, eager to get airborne. Quimby emerged from the hanger dressed in her now-famous plum-colored outfit, fingering her lucky jewelry, as if to waken the good spirit that resided within the amulet. Immediately, reporters rushed to her, all looking for a statement from the most famous woman pilot in the world. She spoke softly while the

Fig. 4-4, Harriet in a studio photo.

Fig. 4-5, Harriet Quimby ready for take off.

reporters busily scribbled her words on their note pads, their heads leaned toward Harriet, working very hard at the art of listening. Harriet graciously answered all the questions, giving particular attention to those concerning the technical parts of her flying machine. Quimby ended the plane-side interview by assuring reporters a forced landing was out of the question. "I have no intention of coming down in the water. I'm a cat, and I don't like the water," she said smiling. With that she climbed the steps to the cockpit. With a dramatic flair, Harriet tossed her cape to Stevens, waved to the crowd and stepped into the pilot's seat. See Fig. 4-5.

Her mechanic made a last-minute inspection of the warping mechanism under the fuselage. While Hardy poked around under the plane, A. Leo Stevens had a few words with Willard. The mechanic stuck his head out from under the airplane. He had a big smile on his oil-spotted face. Everything was okay. With Willard seated comfortably in the back, Quimby gave the signal and her mechanic pulled the propeller through one turn. Quimby flipped a switch, the mechanic spun the propeller, and the seven-cylinder engine sputtered. Hardy put all his weight into the next spin of the propeller. The engine choked and sputtered as the cylinders each fired. The propeller whirled to life. The plane was shaking as the powerful rotary engine tried to pull the plane forward. Four men held the machine by the horizontal stabilizer and landing gear as it strained at the invisible leash. Quimby pushed the throttle, increasing the gas flow to the engine. The men holding the plane felt the increased power developing and dug their heels into the soft earth. Quimby tested the rudder pedals. Hardy, standing in the front and to the side of the propeller waved the okay. She then tested the warping lever and looked at the wings. Quimby was satisfied the mechanical features of the plane were all working satisfactorily. She waited another ten seconds, making sure that the motor was running correctly. Quimby then smiled, raised her right hand in a thumbs-up position, giving the okay signal to the men. They all let go of the airplane and Harriet was immediately into her takeoff roll. Moments later, the Bleriot lifted gracefully into the air and Quimby and her passenger headed for the 27-mile course around the Boston Light. See Fig. 4-6.

The outbound flight was uneventful and about twelve minutes later she flew past the Boston Light. With a gentle touch on the rudder, and a

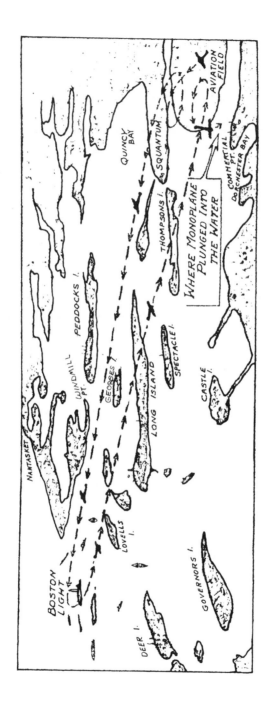

Fig. 4-6, The Boston Globe artist rendition of Harriet Quimby's last flight.

slight warp of the wings, Quimby came out of a descending turn around the lighthouse. She was at an altitude of 2,000 feet. The sun was beginning to set, turning the sky a brilliant orange. Everyone was in awe of the sunset and watched the silhouette of the dragonfly-like monoplane against the fiery sky. Suddenly the plane's tail rose sharply. Willard was thrown out of the craft, his body in an arc that quickly turned to a vertical fall.

Harriet was not immediately award that Willard had fallen from the plane. She was, however, instantly aware that the balance of the plane had shifted. Quimby fought for control, pulling back on the elevate stick to pull the nose up. This had never happened to her before. The craft began to respond to her command. The nose was coming up and for a moment the monoplane seemed to slide back toward a normal attitude.

From the ground it appeared that Quimby had regained control of the craft. A split second later, the monoplane's tail pitched up again like a bucking bronco in a rodeo. The plane was standing on its nose. As the plane went perpendicular, Quimby's body seemed to catapult from her seat. The plane continued rolling over on its back and began falling toward the bay. Thoughts of beauty disappeared as five thousand horrified people watched as Willard and Quimby tumbled through the air and plunged into the harbor waters 200 feet from shore.

The crowd suddenly hushed. Then screams ran through the throng as the reality of the horror unfolded before them. Many covered their faces, unwilling to look. Others watched, riveted to the tragedy that was unfolding before them. Only after the bodies had disappeared beneath the spray of water did the crowd break from the stands.

At the time, the tide was low and the water was only four feet deep where they landed. Later, autopsies revealed that Quimby died on impact, and Willard drowned. Ironically, the Bleriot monoplane flew itself out of the dive, and glided into the water. As the plane's wheels touched the water, it tripped on its landing gear, nosed over on its back but sustained little damage.[10] Later examination of Quimby's aneroid barometer showed that she had reached an altitude of 5,000 feet. See Fig. 4-7.

A. Leo Stevens, Harriet's beau witnessed the tragedy and papers described him as "prostrate with grief." Willard's son, who by the random

Fig. 4-7, The wreckage of Harriet Quimby's monoplane.

flip of a coin could have been the victim was described in "uncontrollable anguish" after witnessing his father fall to his death.

The suddenness of the accident left the people on the ground sickened and in shock. The pilots in the air were not much better off. Blanche Scott, who was airborne and witnessed the tragedy, had difficulty landing her plane. The New York *Times* reported, "With an effort plainly visible from the earth, she started to descend and each time started to falter. In another moment, summoning all her courage, she turned the nose of her machine downward. Then she [Scott] came to a landing like a flash, and collapsed in her seat before anyone could reach her."

Scott later said she tried to land immediately, but the crowd running across the field toward the accident prevented her landing. "A dozen people would have been cut down by my propeller," she said. "They were running in every direction, all over the field."

After Quimby's tragic death, Scott was one of the few remaining women pilots in America. However, she was not to be intimidated by the accident. "I shall make [the remaining] flights according to the schedule," she told a reporter who wondered aloud if she was scared off by the accident. "The tragic death of Harriet Quimby will not deter me. All aviators get here eventually. If they stay in the game, it is only a question of time before something goes wrong, and they die. We all realize that. All aviators are fatalists. They realize what will be, will be."[11]

Ruth Law was also at the Boston Air Meet and watched Harriet Quimby fall to her death. She had just enrolled in a flying school, and had taken her first lesson earlier that day. Quimby's death did not stop Law either. She had tasted a sense of fulfillment in flying, and would not return to the traditional role defined by society. "I purchased a Wright biplane because it seemed to me they had the greatest success. Harriet died in a monoplane but that didn't scare me. I figured it was the monoplane's fault."[12]

After the accident, officials canceled the remainder of the day's program. But in the tradition of show business, the air meet continued the next day. The only reminders of the tragedy were the streamers of black crepe tied to the flying wires of the airplanes and the black arm bands worn by the pilots. The accident greatly reduced attendance and the meet eventually closed $30,000 in debt. Seven aviators had their licenses suspended by the Aero Club for participating in what the club called an unsanctioned event.[13]

In late June, Quimby had received a permit from the Post Office. She would be the first woman to fly the mail. She was going to fly mail from Boston to New York to show the potential for fast mail delivery by air. The experiment was to take place on July 7 as the closing act to the Meet. Stevens had built this into his negotiations. This of course, did not happen, and it would be another year before Marjorie Stinson would garner the honor of being the first woman to fly the mail.[14]

Chapter 5

Aftermath

"With the establishment of fuel supply and landing stations, there is no reason we cannot have airlines for distances of 50 to 60 miles. This mode of travel would be delightful during the summer, allowing one to escape the heat and dust that make overland travel so uncomfortable."- Harriet Quimby, 1911

Harriet Quimby's death raised a storm of criticism in the aviation community, and with the public. All the strong feelings spilled over into the press after her death. Some commentaries were critical because society let a woman fly. Others were sympathetic because she was a female victim of an activity in which she did not belong. Some people even mourned her as just a young person with talent, enthusiasm, and ideas - one who had died before she had lived a full life.

The New York *Sun* commented on her tragic death. "Miss Quimby is the fourth woman in the world killed while operating an aeroplane and their number thus far is four too many. The sport is not one for which women are physically qualified. As a rule they lack strength and presence of mind and the courage to excel as aviators. It is essentially a man's sport and pastime. In the world's now long list of aviation fatalities, none has caused more profound grief in the country than the tragic death of Miss Quimby." Quimby was the second American woman to die in an air accident. Julia Clark's death preceded Quimby's by two weeks when her biplane clipped some trees on takeoff. The craft fell to earth, and the motor mounted behind the pilot's seat broke loose and crushed her. Clark had been the first woman to complete a flying course at the Curtiss Aviation School in San Diego. She had earned her license in a Wright-type biplane on May 19, 1912, after flying in fifteen mile per hour winds to an altitude of 800 feet. Her landing, the officials said, was perfect.[1]

While a maelstrom of criticism whirled around Harriet's tragic death, funeral services were held on the evening of July 4, 1912, at the funeral parlor of Frank E. Campbell, on West 23rd Street in New York City - not far from where she had lived. A large crowd of friends attended the services. Among the mourners were representatives from the Italian Aero Club (of which Quimby was an honorary member) and members of the Aeronautical Society of America. Her friends from *Leslie's Weekly* also attended. The Reverend James Wasson read from the Book of Revelation and said in part, "But in our sorrow tonight there rests still a joyful note. For we realize that through this death there has come progress, and that therefore, Miss Quimby's life was a victory over those elements, which brought on her very end. Through her we reach nearer to the far off goal of our hope. Her name is added to the long list of those who have freely given their lives so the world might be greater and grander."[2] The following day Miss Quimby was laid to rest in Woodland Cemetery on Staten Island. Harriet had feared that her body would be used for experimental purposes and had left instructions that her body be sealed in a copper-covered burglar-proof vault.[3] The mystery of her life followed her to the grave. There was no birth date placed on her headstone. One newspaper in San Francisco where Quimby had worked a decade earlier eloquently commented on her passing with a poem dedicated to her memory:

Rare girl of pencraft, on Bleriot's wings,
Serene and smiling, lady unafraid.
You soared above the groundlings of your trade,
Braving that fate which fate remorseless flings.
But you with vision, courage, flew afar;
Your mentor was the strong-winged Albatross.[4]

At the time of Quimby's death the hydrogen-filled airship, *Akron,* exploded in midair and crashed, killing four men. Calvin Vanimen, the pilot, was flying the craft on a trial run before his attempt at an Atlantic Ocean crossing. On the page in the New York *Times* carrying the Quimby obituary was an expression of sympathy from New York's Governor Woodrow Wilson for Vaniman and the other three airmen who died in the crash. However, sympathy messages for Quimby were strikingly absent.

The ghouls were keeping a score of the tragedies, hoping that when the numbers became unacceptable the public would decide to stop this foolishness called flying. *Leslie's Weekly,* although a strong supporter of Quimby, published the list of victims of aviation's age of innocence. Quimby's death halfway through the year had brought the number of deaths to 43 for 1912, against 73 for all 1911. The trend, if it continued, would produce more deaths than the previous year. The newspaper added that since 1908, 154 Americans had lost their lives in aviation accidents. But the ghouls and statistics would not stem the on-rushing progress the airplane would bring.

An Avoidable Accident

Glenn Martin, a noted aircraft designer, felt that Quimby's accident was preventable. "Miss Quimby's accident would not have happened if they were wearing straps. When going at a terrific speed, the machine on striking a 'hole in the air' will drop suddenly and lift one from his seat. I wear straps on my aeroplane and even then I am thrown violently up against them by such drops."[5] It is ironic that in the June 6, 1912 issue of *Leslie's Weekly,* Harriet wrote a column illustrated with photographs showing the latest in aviation improvements. One photo showed a shoulder harness being worn by some European pilots, to be an early version of the seat belt-harness apparatus worn in today's cars.

The Boston *Globe* also said, "There were many on the field who felt that Mr. Willard had no business making the flight under the circumstances. He had been under heavy strain for several months getting the arrangements for the air meet in place. He was nervous, high-strung, and filled with financial anxiety. His friends felt that it would be better for him not to make the flight . . .."

Fig.5-1, Harriet seen here priming her engine.

The *Globe* quickly assigned the cause of the accident to the lack of seat belts. ". . . had Miss Quimby before taking off buckled the broad strap in the space in front of her, the space from the back of her seat to the strap measured less than a foot, and it is unfathomable that Miss Quimby could have been thrown from her seat without first unbuckling the strap."[6] The reporter did not mention the strap for Willard in the back seat. From today's perspective clearly the reporter knew little about physical forces acting upon a body when the vehicle in which the body is traveling makes a sudden change in direction or speed. One also must remember the strap in Quimby's plane was not a seat belt, but merely meant to retard forward motion.

It was common in those days for pilots not to wear seatbelts. The low-powered aircraft developed comparatively little centrifugal force. Pilots of the day did not go through the excessive and violent maneuvers so commonplace in the later years of aviation. Inverted flight, the popular loop-the-loop, and "yank and bank" turns only evolved as the more powerful and better constructed aircraft came along.

A. Leo Stevens said he believed the accident was the cause of "Willard suddenly straining forward to speak to Miss Quimby." Stevens, a good friend of the Wright Brothers, was familiar with the hazards of flight. He also said he warned Willard twice before the flight not to move around or leave his seat under any circumstances. "This warning I was very particular to give," he said, "because I knew him to be a man of sudden impulses. Many times talking with him I have known him to leap from his seat to tell me of an idea that suddenly came to him. I believe that as they were coming back to the landing field, Willard, who weighed 190 pounds, had an enthusiastic moment for Miss Quimby's splendid performance. For a moment he forgot the danger of moving, and suddenly stretched forward or stood up to shout words of congratulations to Miss Quimby. She was about three feet forward, but in doing so, upset the delicate balance." (The hood on the machine separating the pilot from the passenger had been removed to make Quimby's access easier. Between her and the passenger there were just two boards.) "Miss Quimby had no way of seeing Willard moving forward, no warning of the shift in balance, and therefore no time to take corrective action." Stevens' theory had some validity, according to the Boston Aeronautical Society.

They said the cause of the accident was "lack of fore and aft stability to counteract rotation on the center of gravity of the machine."

Quimby was a hero to millions of people, but this tragedy gave people time to refocus on the role of women in aviation. Some used her tragic death to prove that women were physically and psychologically unfit to fly. Lincoln Beachey, a well-known aviator, had a typical analysis of her tragedy. The Boston *Globe* published his comments. "Miss Quimby was coming down from five thousand feet with full power. The machine was wobbling in the gusty breeze. She was a light, delicate woman and it could easily have happened that the terrific rush of air was too much for her and that she became weakened and unable to control her levers." (Beachey was a reckless pilot who could not comprehend a woman flying. He was the first pilot to loop-the-loop, and in the end, his daring cost him his life. In 1915, he failed to recover the aircraft from a loop, the wings crumpled from the stress and he crashed into the ground.)

"Before starting her flight, her mechanic gave her instructions regarding pumping gasoline from the auxiliary tank to the main tank," continued Beachey. "She had to reach forward to do this as there was a two or three-way valve she had to turn before starting to pump. She did not seem very familiar with the operation or the exact way to turn the valve before and after pumping. Her gasoline may have become low in the main tank and she may have attempted to pump some in from the auxiliary. She may have become confused on which way to turn the valve. Realizing her engine was liable to stop, she may have attempted to come down at a steeper angle and land. She was in a very good position to do this nicely."[7]

Stevens angrily disputed Beachey's claim by citing Miss Quimby's instantaneous attempt to right the machine. He also said, "As her manager and her close friend, I knew her to be a woman of great coolness and judgement, and a pilot of extraordinary ability. With Willard's weight gone - a weight absolutely necessary to the control of the monoplane - she was up against circumstances over which no aviator, no human ingenuity, knowledge, skill, or practice could have controlled."[8]

The renowned British aviator Claude Grahame-White, whose record Quimby was attempting to break, pondered the question put forth by the Detroit *Free Press* "Ought Women to Aviate?" It took him seconds to answer, citing Quimby as an example. Women, he said, are "temperamentally unfit for flight because they are prone to panic. When calamity overtakes my women pupils as eventually I fear it will, I shall feel in a way responsible for their sudden decease." Grahame-White was an opportunist and took advantage of the situation. He opposed women flying, but contradicted himself and accepted them as students because he needed the money for the high maintenance expenses of his airplane.

Paul Peck, another flyer, had another analysis. "She was coming down with the power wide open and when she threw the tail up to 'volplane' (dive) in, Willard was not expecting it and was thrown out and she followed about one or two hundred feet later. The machine struck the water at a perfect gliding angle, wheels first. I am positive from the way in which it came down and from my later examination that nothing went wrong with the controls. Had they been wearing straps this would never have happened."[9]

Andre Houpert, Quimby's instructor and friend, also had something to say. His impressions evidently reflected the product of an impartial mind, and backed by years of experience. He also had the simplicity of a man who was real, coupled with the charm of a cultured Frenchman. "Flying is a profession that has shot more stars into the firmament of fame than any other in a comparative space of time, only to blot them out more quickly than any other. The only man on earth who came closest to knowing what happened to Miss Quimby was her mechanic, and I talked to him yesterday. He worked for months with her, he knew her ways and the machine, and there was nothing wrong with the flying capacity of either.

"I have never known Miss Quimby to be without nerve, but I think she was getting a little tired of it. It seems to me she was getting less enthusiastic than I had known her to be at first."[10]

Typically at the scene of a tragedy eyewitness accounts differed. The Boston *Globe* quickly quoted several other experts who were advancing their own interests. Their theories, however, were conflicting. Earle Ovington, another leading pilot of the day, claimed Willard had appointed him assistant manager of the Meet just ten minutes before the ill-fated flight. He also claimed that he was the first to reach the crash site. He said he found that the rudder control wire caught over the lower end of the vertical control lever used to warp the wings. "This," he said, "caused the machine to turn left and pitch headmost downward catapulting the occupants out." Ovington said unequivocally that the jammed controls caused the accident. The jamming sequence began when Miss Quimby moved the vertical warping lever sharply to the right, probably to correct for a gust of wind that struck her on the starboard side." Ovington also claimed he saw exactly what had happened in the sky. "I saw the machine swerve to the left and dip downward, not, however, at a very great angle. Immediately Willard was thrown out and clear of the machine and a fraction of a second later Quimby followed." Others had claimed that Willard had jumped because of the apparent great distance in which the body had traveled, but Ovington disputed this. " If Willard had jumped, he would have been thrown only about 2-3 feet instead of 25 feet. Put two pennies on a ruler, some distance from each other. Rotate the ruler on its axis until the pennies fly off. The penny farthest from the axis go father. Miss Quimby had the warping control lever between her legs and the control wheel to grasp; her grasp would have been broken with more difficulty than Willard's."

Ovington claimed that a wind hit the right side of the craft causing Quimby to move the upper end of the warping lever to the right. This would warp the right wing and cause the left wing to rise. With this motion, Ovington claimed a loose rudder wire became caught on the warping wire and caused loss of control. He said that covering the rudder wire or isolating it would prevent a repeat of this accident. Ovington also claimed that he had flown 107 flights in a similar machine and, ". . . had never broken a stick on the machine."[11]

While he admitted the evidence was strongly circumstantial, Ovington placed the blame on two people. He said, "I know the machine Miss Quimby flew, having flown many hundreds of miles in one myself. The cause of the accident was not Miss Quimby's but the blame should be placed on the doorstep of the designer." He also fixed some of the blame on her faithful mechanic, Hardy, who could have kept the wires tighter.

The *Boston Globe* reported Quimby's French mechanic became "wrathy" when Ovington stated his theory to bystanders, including her loyal mechanic, only minutes after Quimby's body was recovered. Hardy had his simple, unscientific, but accurate theory: "Too steep a glide," he said. "The machine lost its balance." He was sure there was no mechanical failure. "I personally tested every screw, bolt, and wire before I pushed the machine from the hanger. I always did that. I never let Miss

Quimby get in the seat much less carry a passenger unless I was satisfied that every part of the machine was perfect. But what could have happened? I can only say what has always happened to Bleriot monoplanes. Most accidents to Bleriot types have happened usually always alike. They have all lost their balance."

The *Evening Globe* called in other experts who disputed Ovington's theory. Experts claimed to have examined the wreckage and said that "after a careful examination of that part of the machine this morning with a full knowledge of Ovington's theory in mind, our experts [not named] didn't verify his findings." A photograph with the article illustrated the apparent errors in Mr. Ovington's conclusions.

To discredit Ovington's contention that a loose wire had caused the accident, the *Evening Globe* wrote, "This morning that selfsame experiment was tried and we found that the wires . . . failed to come anywhere near the tip of the vertical rod. With that theory disproved, various experiments with the vertical post, the rudder and warping wires, and the elevating wires also failed to show a cause. The rudder wires, controlled by the feet, in no way conflicted with the wires leading to the elevator. The warping wires were also safely removed from possible contact with the other sets."

A day later the *Boston Globe* added some credibility to the mechanic's theory: "It appears that accidents similar to this have occurred often in France - always with fatal results and nearly always in the Bleriot monoplane. The French government is studying this kind of accident with the Bleriot monoplane, and they allege it to be due to the curve at the entrant edge of the plane's wing." The *Globe* also mentioned that John Moisant had been flying a monoplane "modeled after the Bleriot's most up-to-date design when he plunged headforemost to earth."

The Technical Explanation

In August 1912, *Aircraft* magazine devoted four pages to the accident. One article by Walter H. Phipps, "The Danger of the Lifting Tail and its Probable Bearing on the Death of Miss Quimby," convincingly argued the dangerous instability of that monoplane design. Phipps pointed out that the fixed horizontal tail surface of the small two-seat plane was a small cambered wing set at a higher lifting angle (to help carry the weight of a passenger who sat well behind the plane's center of gravity), very similar to the craft's main lifting wing. "A machine of this type," he wrote, "has not the slightest degree of automatic longitudinal stability and . . . is an extremely tricky and dangerous type to handle. The horizontal tail should act as a stabilizing damper, preventing the machine from either diving too steeply or stalling and not under any circumstances as a lifting plane . . . it must be either a flat or slightly negatively inclined surface." He explained that in a certain nose-down angle (caused by a gust of wind or carelessness of the pilot), the tail gains in lift as the speed increases, until reaching the critical angle and speed. "Then," he wrote, "it is impossible to get the tail down though the elevator stick is pulled back. The faster the machine dives, the more lift the tail provides until it has the plane in a vertical position hurling the pilot and passenger out (unless they are strapped in)." Phipps listed in his article almost a dozen pilots who died in Bleriot monoplanes under similar circumstances where the plane dove straight into the ground.[12] He does not say if any of the victims fell from the craft as did Quimby and Willard.

Witnesses began to hurl opinions and theories around like rice at a wedding. The pilot had vertigo; the plane's fuselage snapped in half (there was no evidence of this); a violent downrush of air pushed the plane into the bay. More dubious and unprovable theories came forward. Many voiced their opinions on why Quimby's plane went out of control, tossing her and Willard to their deaths. One opinion was that Willard's wife had recently died, and he was so despondent that he jumped from the plane and upset the delicate balance. Others said the wings had dipped too sharply causing a severe strain and part of the mechanism gave way. Some said Quimby was not in good health and was overcome while controlling the high-powered machine.

With today's knowledge of aeronautic science, Phipps' analysis seems to be the most accurate assessment. Whatever one chooses to believe - too steep a glide, a gust of wind, the broken rudder wire or the lifting tailplane - the Bleriot monoplane was a terribly unforgiving aircraft, even for pilots like Harriet Quimby who had more experience in the type than most pilots of the day. In hindsight, Harriet Quimby and her unsuspecting passenger were truly victims of aviation's age of innocence.

The Future for Women

Before her death, Quimby had written an article giving her opinion of aviation as a career for women. The article for *Good Housekeeping Magazine* did not appear until September, two months after her fatal plunge. "I think," she said, "there is no reason the aeroplane should not open a fruitful occupation for women. I see no reason they cannot realize handsome incomes by carrying passengers between adjacent towns, from parcel delivery, taking photographs, or conducting schools of flying. Any of these things it is now possible to do. The number of men fliers will always outnumber the women, just as chauffeurs outnumber the women who drive automobiles. With the establishment of fuel supply and landing stations, there is no reason we cannot have airlines for distances of 50 to 60 miles. This mode of travel would be delightful during the Summer, allowing one to escape the heat and dust that make overland travel so uncomfortable."

The anonymous editor added a preface to Miss Quimby's article, "In view of her tragic death, there is a note of pathos in the enthusiasm and in the prophecy for women fliers in her article."[13]

Like the graceful and strong-winged albatross, Harriet Quimby had charted a course for women over uncharted waters. She had the endurance and strength of the great sea bird and like her mentor pressed on despite the seemingly overwhelming journey that lay before her.

And like a meteor, Harriet Quimby had streaked through the skies and her show was breathtaking in its brilliance. But as suddenly as a meteor appears, it is gone. Quimby was gone and the skies over America suddenly seemed empty with her passing. In the short time she had left a legacy for women and science, but Harriet Quimby had not survived the first anniversary of her license.

Two weeks after her death *Leslie's Weekly* wrote an inspired editorial tribute to her, commenting on her talent:

A brilliant light in the literary firmament has been extinguished. The tragic death of Miss Harriet Quimby, the most famous aviatrice, while flying with a passenger at the Air Meet, put a sad and sudden end to a career that promised for literature, art, and science.

Miss Quimby conducted the dramatic department of Leslie's an independence and fairness that won general admiration. critical art reviews

Fig. 5-2, This photo of Harriet Quimby celebrated her Channel flight and found its way onto the inside cover of a cigar box.

were marvels of style and expression, while a writer on aeronautics she was one with the highest

She took up aviation less than two years ago, first it was pastime, but afterward because she became devoted to development of the science. She firmly believed aeronautics much for the progress of the century, and gave her young life as sacrifice to a sense of duty. The staff of Leslie's, with whom had been a willing, helpful, faithful worker and associate for past ten years, feel her loss as few others can. But they have comfort of many assurances from her lips that, in her inmost she felt no fear of death because she remained serene in the that it would open the door to a fadeless immortality.

Quimby's articles continued to appear in *Leslie's Weekly* for two issues after her death, and the scope of her talent is seen in the variety of subjects she covered. During her career she wrote more than 250 articles and they covered topics like, "Can Women Run Automobiles?" and a critical review of an opera called, "Through the Opera Glass."

When the editor began the solitary and sorrowful task of removing Harriet's personal belonging from her desk he discovered an unfinished article she had been preparing. The article, titled "Lost in the Sky" along with the editor's comments were published in the November 28, 1912 issue of *Leslie's Weekly*.

"There is something pathetic and prophetic in the unfinished manuscript," said the editor, "found on the desk of the late Harriet Quimby, the aviatrice who fell to her death at the Boston meet last July. Miss Quimby had prepared the data for an article for *Leslie's* relating to her experiences while lost in her monoplane during flights in Mexico, Garden City and other places. She had written the opening pages of the story. They are the last words she left for her readers in *Leslie's*, to whom she sent her helpful messages every week. As they have a singular interest in connection with her sad and untimely death, we print them herewith. The simple caption on the article, as written by her, was one word, "Lost!" How soon was fate to find its fulfillment! The unfinished manuscript reads as follows:

Nobody likes to be lost. There is a wretchedness about it most pathetic. Our hearts go out to the lost child, we join in the search for the missing.

Whether we be strangers or neighbors. The instinct to go to the rescue is always the same.

It is a new experience to be lost in the sky, but it is as real and as trying as to be lost in the midst of earth's wilderness or on the infinite expanse of the waters of the sea. I speak with knowledge. Twice I have been lost while driving a monoplane.

The sense of loneliness and helplessness one feels while driving a thousand feet above the earth in a swiftly moving monoplane, with nothing but everlasting sky above and the horizon around and with no signs of recognition from the distant earth below, is overwhelming and indescribable. One can do nothing but look and hope. One must drive on, amid the roar of the motor blade making its thousand revolutions a minute.

The aviator who is lost feels no helping hand reach out to him. He looks for none. There is nothing to do except keep an eye keenly on the watch for some friendly meadow or spread of water, indicating the location of the aviation field to which a safe descent can be made. But it is never hopeless, for the aviator knows that if darkness supervenes, it will, in all probability, disclose the beacon fires of watchers on the field. If one has not flown too far away, he can easily recognize, from his commanding place of vantage, the blazing pile where the watchers wait.

Why should I be lost in the air? It is the easiest thing in the world. The landmarks you see, as you walk or ride on the surface of the earth, are not recognized as such by the flyer. On the earth you see these things straight ahead or to the side, within the horizontal range of the eye. From a balloon or an aeroplane you see the roof, not the sides of the house; pinnacles that pierce the sky, not the majestic towers that command the vision from the side view.

Recall your own experience and your exclamations of surprise after you have gone to the top of the Washington Monument at the national capital, the Arch d'Triumphe in Paris, the top of Bunker Hill at Boston, or of a skyscraper in any city. You find yourself puzzled as to the points of the compass. The most familiar buildings, streets and avenues are almost indistinguishable except as you study the vista spread before you.

It is a wonder that one gets lost in the sky? Remember that from the dizzy height of a monoplane as one looks over the side of a car, the earth seems flattened out, rivers shrink until they become no larger than brooks, the hills are leveled and fields of variegated color appear like spaces on a checkerboard. The earth is flat, not round, as the aeroplanist sees it. But I could always pick my landing at any time when I was lost, for I kept sailing about until I found a suitable place. Then I came down and was happy!

The closing sentence," the editor said, "of this last unfinished manuscript of Miss Quimby's recalls a sealed message she left for her parents before she went to Boston to make her last flight. In that message, which carried with it a sad premonition, she said that if ill fortune should befall her, she would meet her fate "rejoicing."

Surely this brave girl, the first in the United States to secure a pilot's license to fly, deserves a fitting memorial. We are glad to say that contributions to her Monument Fund are still being received by us."

The August 8, 1912 issue of *Leslie's Weekly* claimed that hundreds of dollars were pouring in with letters suggesting that a monument be erected to Miss Quimby's memory in Woodlawn Cemetery. The letters, the paper said, included contributions from $1 upward and spoke of Miss Quimby's rare personal qualities and of her remarkable courage in displaying her faith in the science of aviation. The memorial monument was completed in June 1913 and placed on her grave. The inscription reads:

Harriet Quimby
The First woman in America to receive a pilot's license to fly. The first woman in the world to fly a monoplane alone across the English Channel April 16, 1912.
The life of the heroic girl went out when she fell with her passenger aeroplane at Boston July 1, 1912. She was Dramatic Editor of Leslie's Weekly.
Rest Gentle Spirit

Fig. 5-3, The 1991 stamp honoring Harriet Quimby.

Ganesha Legend

Harriet Quimby's death quickly took on a mystical quality, and the superstitious have blamed it on the jewelry she wore. From the start of her flying career, Quimby had been the most flamboyant personality in aviation circles at the time. Harriet had a flair for the dramatic and wore certain jewelry on every flight. It shows up in almost all her photographs. This jewelry has become a legend - the legend of her misfortune.

During her trip to Mexico, Harriet bought a bracelet and necklace alleged to be a 2,000 year-old piece of Aztec jewelry. It had an Aztec head made from clay, and attached to an antique silver chain. She had also picked up an East Indian idol called *Ganesha* on her trip to London just before her Channel flight. Legend has it that the idol brought bad luck to its former owner, a French pilot. Before she had bought this idol, people said her life was orderly and filled with good fortune. Harriet wore the jewelry on her Channel flight and the spirit within seemed to provide its protective cloak. She had also tied *Ganesha* to the monoplane during the flight. Coincidentally, on her return to America from her Channel flight, some people say her luck changed. She had disappointments, and misfortune. Eleanor Trehawke-Davis, who flew the English Channel as a passenger just before Quimby, later died in an air accident. The jewelry took on a macabre touch when people found that Harriet had lent the ornaments to Mrs. Davis. After Quimby's death, the jewelry disappeared. The story goes her mother wanted to donate the pieces to the Smithsonian Institution but they disappeared from the body. So the legend developed that the possessor of the tusk jewelry would have ill fortune. The lost jewelry perhaps still brings its errant owners misfortune.

Just two days before her tragic death, Quimby had written an article describing, half-whimsically, the bad luck the little idol *Ganesha* was bringing her. *World Magazine* published the piece two weeks after her death, on July 14, 1912.

It is a curious thing but all women flyers are superstitious. And again it isn't so curious either. All people who follow a calling in which chance enters largely are superstitious. My superstition is Ganesha, a little ancient brass idol.

He brought me such bad luck and was such a misbehaved person that I simply had to kill him. So he had his little brass head sawed off and he's been wonderfully behaved ever since. You must not laugh when I tell you that I think there is something to the little beast. He looked so grumpy and so eery that he used to give me the shivers, although the beast was quite likable at first. The idol had an elephant head, on a man-like body, with two legs crossed and a third leg very conveniently stuck out of his elbow. He also had three arms, all busy, and a very fat stomach. Unlike Buddha, who sits and broods over the earth, Ganesha showed the potential for a lively disposition. One hand held an axe, another a hook, and the third a stone. The free foot looked as if it might kick out from the shoulder at any moment. Another reporter described Ganesha in political satire. Considering the elephant head, the axe with which to cut himself, the hook to give himself, the mud to sling and the foot to oust the contested delegates, he was not unlike a complete Republican Party.

When first I saw him it was in the office of the London Daily Mirror. He was in with other talisman and idols who had brought their owners bad luck. The Daily Mirror decided to round up these misbegotten omens of ill-luck. Thousands poured in from all over the city. This Saturday afternoon when I retrieved the little brass idol he was ready for the funeral pyre. At the time I did not know of his unsavory past.

I tied him to my Bleriot on my Channel crossing. As I said he was so likable at first, I wished him to be my good luck charm, but I also wore my jewelry. Perhaps he was the cause of the foul weather over the Channel and my difficulty with the engine. Thinking back my lucky jewelry probably neutralized his power during my flight.[14]

Quimby later found out the idol had belonged to a French aviator who met some reverses. He gave the brass god to a country gentleman, who also suffered misfortunes and surrendered him to the *Daily Mirror*.

Quimby tried to keep her flight a secret until it was completed.

This is where the Ganesha got his first licks. I am sure he worked against me in that regard too. Two days later the aviator (I will not mention his name) took a woman as a passenger across the Channel, taking from me the distinction of being the first woman to cross. As you know, I was the first to make the flight alone, but the other should have been mine too had it not been for my little brass friend. I am sure my jewelry largely counteracted my malevolent little friend.

After the flight, the man who promised me $5,000 for the flight went back on his word [the editor at the London Daily Mirror]. I had heard so much of the British solidity and business honor that I could not think of making a written contract with him. Disgusted I left for America. Ganesha came along too, because I did not suspect anything, at least not at the time.

No sooner than Quimby had landed, she had small disputes, the first on how to classify her new aeroplane in Customs in New York. Following this were financial disputes, none of them serious, but all annoying and unpleasant. "In the past two months, she said, "I have seen my lawyer about thirty times. Before that I don't remember talking over matters with him ten times in a year."

Soon she began to suspect *Ganesha*. "I believe he meant to do things I accused him of; it seemed to me that way. So I spanked him and set him out as a paper weight, a humiliating position for one so ancient. It was no use. He simply would not behave. His tricks were just as mean and unfriendly. Then I took a hammer to him, but your true aristocrat is tenacious of life and I couldn't dent him anywhere."

Quimby then took strong and irrevocable action. "I decided he should die after holding court over him and rehearsing his evil actions. In this court of convenience, he did not even have the benefit of counsel or a jury trial. He had to die. Afterward I was sorry for him, but law is law, and the sentence had to be carried out. But how?" Harriet had difficulty figuring out just how to dispatch the little beast.

Obviously he could not be electrocuted or hanged, nor poisoned nor shot for his misbehaved soul was solid brass. In the midst of my problem a reporter suggested that Ganesha should have his head cut off. That is a fitting end for any gentleman, and according to ancient custom quite the proper thing. In the engraving room of the newspaper are some glittering circular saws that go through brass like a knife through cheese.

So I took Ganesha into the darkened engraving room that was to be his death chamber and had a worker hold him in front of the saw. Nervously I noted him lying on the steel table as the saw's sharp teeth tried to do their work.

Suddenly the saw stopped cutting. Ganesha was not willing to die. The workman examined Ganesha. He demanded to know what kind of brass went into this stubborn little aristocrat. I could not tell except that it must be very tough, quite appropriate to Ganesha's disposition. It took two saw blades before the shrieking stopped and his head flew off. He was too hot to touch for awhile, but when I cooled him off in water he seemed a sorry sight.

Now I still have him on my desk as a paper weight. When he behaves he can have his head back, but the minute he starts any of his old tricks I'll take his head away from him.

Since he lost his head a week ago, things have gone splendidly. Now maybe it is, and maybe it isn't, his former influence, but just the same, things are going better. I am going to let him wear his head a full day, sometime soon, to see if I have cured him of his unsavory ways.[15]

Quimby placed the head back on the idol before she left for Boston. The *Ganesha* was sitting, head restored, on her desk at *Leslie's Weekly* when Quimby fell to her death. (There is no record of *Ganesha*'s final disposition but it seems logical that a beheaded brass paper weight idol would quickly find its way to the trash pail, and from there most likely to a watery grave on a garbage barge.)

In Summary

Harriet Quimby was gone, and many people wondered why women like Quimby and others gambled their lives in such unreliable, unstable and unpredictable machines. There are two reasons: first, no one, male or female, really knew how a stable aircraft should act. There was very little scientific knowledge. Testing and aircraft design in 1912 was mainly by ear and by eye, with trial and error experience. But Amelia Earhart later summed up the real reason. Before her last flight Earhart wrote to her husband, "I want to do it because I want to do it. Women must try to do things as men have tried. When they fail, their failure must be but a challenge to others."[16]

Debates about the issue of women in aviation went on for years afterward, and continue to this day. Women not only began flying shortly after men did, but from the beginning made creative contributions like Quimby. Women continued flying after Quimby's death, braving the same hazards as the men, exploring the limits of mechanical and human endurance.

Harriet Quimby had calmly matched wits with the best of the men, but refused to be like them. She showed the world that her courage and determination matched the best of the best. She reluctantly acquiesced to many feminine mores of her day, but refused to be enslaved by them. Although she went down in history as another aviation statistic accumulated during "aviation's age of innocence," Harriet Quimby courageously opened the door to the great women pilots who followed her. Women like Amelia Earhart saw the opportunity for freedom and followed Quimby's lead. They began asserting themselves in the air and on the ground.

Quimby's spirit was no doubt angered by the editorials criticizing her judgement, her "invasion" of the private fraternity of male aviation, and her skill. More than 80 years later, time has vindicated Harriet. If Harriet were here today she would smile and rejoice, and point upward to women flying military jets and commercial airliners, saying, "See, I told you so!"

Harriet Quimby, most will agree, died in the prime of her life and at the peak of her career. One can only speculate on how far she would have led women in her quest for equality on the ground and in the air. Perhaps she would have been the first person to solo the Atlantic. She would have gladly accepted the challenge. And maybe she would have been the first person to solo around the world. There is no doubt she had the courage. She had confidence in her abilities and she was possessed with persistence, determination and self-esteem. Her eleven months of achievements in the air were enough to imprint her indelibly in the fabric of American history. She was obsessed with the compulsion to write everything she had seen and experienced. Like Keats she seemed to ". . . have fears that I may cease to be before my pen has gleaned my teaming brain."

Fig. 5-4 The three stamps honoring American women pilots.

Harriet was not born rich or tutored abroad but never denied the fiction. Why? In reality Quimby struggled to gain a common public school education. And why, at the time of her death did she claim to be 28, when she was actually 37? These questions will always remain a mystery, but do they not merely enhance her achievements?

Afterword

A. Leo Stevens mourned Harriet's death for more than a year. In October 1913, at the request of her mother, Stevens had his one true love's remains removed from Woodlawn Cemetery and reinterred in the Quimby family plot in Kensico Cemetery in Valhalla, New York.

Ursula Quimby, Harriet's mother passed away in 1916, and is buried in the family's plot with her daughter. Her father, William Quimby, passed away in 1922, at the age of 87, and is buried in what he considered his hometown of Greenville, Michigan.

Quimby's closest friend and confidante, Matilde Moisant, never flew in air shows again after her fiery crash landing, and lived longer than most of her contemporaries, male or female. She folded her wings in 1964, at the age of 77. Like Harriet, even in death, controversy touched Matilde Moisant. Her relatives came forward and claimed she was really 85 years old when she died. (Had Harriet lived as long as Matilde she would have been 89.)

In the more than half century that passed after Harriet's death, Matilde Moisant seldom gave interviews. She left an oral history at Columbia University, and in a rare interview shortly before her death she said, "My flying career did not last very long, because in those days that was man's work, and they didn't think a nice girl should be in it." Moisant never discussed Harriet's private life or the circumstances of her death with anyone. She remained a true friend to the end.

On June 5 1988, the city of Coldwater, Michigan honored the memory of Harriet Quimby by installing a State Marker at the Branch County Airport located in Coldwater.

On April 27, 1991, the Post Office issued a stamp honoring Harriet Quimby. See Fig. 5-3. She is the third American woman aviator to be honored. Blanche Scott and Amelia Earhart are the others. See Fig 5-4.

Appendix

A copy of William and Ursula Quimby's marriage certificate.

Appendix

The Commonwealth of Massachusetts

STANDARD CERTIFICATE OF DEATH

QUINCY
(City or town.)

PLACE OF DEATH

Quincy, Mass. (No. In water off Squantum St.; 6 Ward)

[If death occurred in a hospital or institution, give its NAME instead of street and number.]

FULL NAME Harriet Quimby

[If married or divorced woman or widow give maiden name, also name of husband.]

RESIDENCE New York

Registered No. 246

PERSONAL AND STATISTICAL PARTICULARS	MEDICAL CERTIFICATE OF DEATH
SEX Female **COLOR OR RACE** White **SINGLE, MARRIED, WIDOWED, OR DIVORCED** (Write the word) Single	**DATE OF DEATH** July 1, 1912 (Month) (Day) (Year)
DATE OF BIRTH 1885 (Month) (Day) (Year)	I HEREBY CERTIFY that I have investigated the death of the deceased.
AGE 27 yrs. mos. ds. **If LESS than 1 day hrs. or min. ?**	The CAUSE OF DEATH was as follows:
OCCUPATION (a) Trade, profession, or particular kind of work Special writer	Accidental fall from an aeroplane. Multiple internal injuries and fractures, shock. Immediate death
(b) General nature of industry, business, or establishment in which employed (or employer)	(Duration) yrs. mos. ds.
BIRTHPLACE (State or country) California	Contributory (Secondary)
NAME OF FATHER William Quimby	(Duration) yrs. mos. ds. (Signed) Fred E. Jones, M.D.
BIRTHPLACE OF FATHER (State or country) New York	July 1, 1912 (Address) Quincy, Mass. MEDICAL EXAMINER
MAIDEN NAME OF MOTHER Ursula Cook	* State the DISEASE CAUSING DEATH, or, in deaths from VIOLENT CAUSES, state (1) MEANS of INJURY; and (2) whether ACCIDENTAL, SUICIDAL or HOMICIDAL.
BIRTHPLACE OF MOTHER (State or country) New York	**LENGTH OF RESIDENCE** (FOR HOSPITALS, INSTITUTIONS, TRANSIENTS, OR RECENT RESIDENTS). At place of death yrs. mos. ds. In the State yrs. mos. ds.
THE ABOVE IS TRUE TO THE BEST OF MY KNOWLEDGE (Informant) A. Leo Stevens	Where was disease contracted, if not at place of death? Former or usual residence
(Address) 401 W. 24th St., New York	**PLACE OF BURIAL OR REMOVAL** Woodlawn Cemetery New York City	**DATE OF BURIAL** July 2, 1912
July 3, 1912 Emeline J. Crane REGISTRAR	**UNDERTAKER** John Hall	**ADDRESS** Quincy.

An official copy of Harriet Quimby's death certificate.

Note the error in the year she was born.

Bibliography

Books
- Gertrude Bacon. *Memories of Land and Sea.* London. Methuen & Co., 1928
- Katherine Brooks-Pazmany, *United States Women in Aviation 1919-1929.* Washington: Smithsonian Studies in Air & Space No.5; 1978
- Amelia Earhart. *The Fun of It.* New York: Harcourt Brace, 1932 - Ann Hodgeman and Rudy Djabbaroff. *Skystars - The History of Women in Aviation.* New York. Antheneum, 1981
History of the 99s. Oklahoma City: The 99s Inc., 1979
- Oliver Jensen. *The Revolt of American Women.* New York: Harcourt & Brace Company, 1952
- Charles P. May. *Women in Aeronautics.* New York: Nelson 1962
- Valerie Moolman. *Women Aloft.* New York: Time Life Books, 1981
- Claudia M. Oakes. *United States Women in Aviation Through World War I.* Washington: Smithsonian Studies in Air and Space No.2, 1979
- Betty Peckham, *Women in Aviation.* New York: Thomas Nelson & Sons, Inc., 1945.
- Charles E. Planck. *Women With Wings.* New York: Harper Brothers, 1942
- *Chronicle of the 20th Century.* Mt. Kisco, N.Y.: Chronicle Publications, 1981

Magazine Articles
- Frank Delear, "America's Tragic Queen of the Air." *Aviation Heritage,* January 1991.
_____ "What Killed Harriet Quimby?" *Yankee Magazine,* September, 1979.
- Elizabeth H. Gregory, "Women's Records in Aviation." *Good Housekeeping,* September 1912.
- Minna Ivey, "Call to the Sky," *Leslie's Illustrated Weekly,* October 5, 1911
- Terry Gwynn Jones, "For A Brief Moment The World Seemed Wild About Harriet." *Smithsonian Magazine,* January, 1984.
- Julie Opell Klym, "America's First Flight Academy." *AOPA Pilot,* October 1979.

- Bill McAllister, "Who Knew She Flew." *Washington Post*, April 19, 1991.

- Earle Ovington, "Not Miss Quimby's Fault." *Leslie's Illustrated Weekly*, August 1, 1912.

- Walter H. Phipps, "The Danger of the Lifting Tail and the Probable Bearing on the Death of Harriet Quimby." *Aircraft*, August 1912.

- Frank Potter, "The Swan Song Flight of Miss Matilde." *Aviation Quarterly*, Vol. 5, No. 2.

- Hugh Powell, "Harriet Quimby America's First Woman Pilot." *American Aviation Historical Society Journal*, Winter 1982.

- Harriet Quimby, "A Night At A Haunted House." *Call-Bulletin & Chronicle*, February 2, 1902.

_____"Curious Chinese Customs." *Leslie's Illustrated Weekly*, January 22, 1903.

_____"A Woman's Exciting Ride in A Motor Car." *Leslie's Illustrated Weekly*, October 4, 1906

_____"A Japanese Aeronaut to Startle the World." *Leslie's Illustrated Weekly*, August 5, 1909.

_____"Women Automobile Enthusiasts." *Leslie's Illustrated Weekly*, January 12, 1911

_____"How A Woman Learns to Fly." *Leslie's Illustrated Weekly*, May 25, 1911,

_____"How Can We Save Our Birds." *Leslie's Illustrated Weekly*, June 8, 1911

_____"Exploring the Airlanes." *Leslie's Illustrated Weekly*, June 22, 1911

_____"How A Woman Learns to Fly (Part II)." *Leslie's Illustrated Weekly*, August 17, 1911

_____"How I Won My Aviator's License." *Leslie's Illustrated Weekly*, August 24, 1911.

_____"The Dangers of Flying and How to Avoid Them." *Leslie's Illustrated Weekly*, August 31, 1911

_____"In the World of People Who Fly." *Leslie's Illustrated Weekly*, January 18, 1912

_____"With the Intrepid Flyers." *Leslie's Illustrated Weekly*, March 12, 1912

_____"An American Girl's Daring Exploit." *Leslie's Illustrated Weekly*, May 16, 1912

_____ "New Things in the Aviation World." *Leslie's Illustrated Weekly,* June 6, 1912

_____ "Flyers and Flying." *Leslie's Illustrated Weekly,* June 27, 1912

_____ "How I Made My First Big Flight Abroad." *FLY Magazine,* June, 1912.

_____ "American Bird Women." *Good Housekeeping,* June 1912

_____ "We Girls Who Fly and What We're Afraid of." *The World Magazine,* July 14, 1912

_____ "Aviation As A Feminine Sport." *Good Housekeeping,* September, 1912.

_____ "Lost in the Sky,"*Leslie's Illustrated Weekly* November 28, 1912

- Elizabeth Roy, "An American Woman's Trip in an Airship." *Leslie's Illustrated Weekly,* May 9, 1912

- Elizabeth Ann Semple, "Harriet Quimby: America's First Woman Aviator." *Overland Monthly* Magazine, San Francisco. December 1911.

- A. Leo Stevens, "On the Death of Miss Quimby." *Aeronautics,* August 1912.

- George Weston, "Beauty and the Bleriot." *Aviation Quarterly,* Vol. 6 No. 1. 1980

- Samuel Whitt, "Miss Harriet Quimby." *National Aeronautics,* September 1973.

- Nancy Zerfoss, "Schoolmarm to School Ms." *Changing Education,* Summer 1974.

Other

- *Congressional Record,* June 4, 1987
- *Air Service Journal,* October 10, 1917
- *Fly,* Vol. 3 September 1911
- *Fly,* Vol. 4, August 1912
- Manistee County Census, June 18, 1880, p.34
- Marriage certificate William and Ursula (Cook) Quimby, dated October 9, 1859.
- Death Certificate, Harriet Quimby dated July 2, 1912

Newspapers
- *Leslie's Weekly,* various
- *New York Times*, various
- *Newsday,* February 7, 1964
- *Staten Islander,* September 7, 1911
- *Boston Globe,* July 2, 1912
- *Evening Globe,* July 2, 1912
- *Daily Courier,* Coldwater, MI. July 3, 1912
- *Call Bulletin & Chronical*, San Francisco, various 1902

Reference Notes

Chapter One
1- Robert Paltock, *The Life and Adventures of Peter Wilkins.* Hyperion Press, 1928. p. 251
2- Ann Hodgeman, Rudy Djabbaroff. *Skystar: History of Women in Aviation.* Atheneum. 1981; p.6
3- Congressional Record, June 4, 1987.
4- Terry Gwynn Jones. "For A Brief Moment The World Seemed Wild About Harriet." *Smithsonian Magazine,* January 1984.
5- Elizabeth Ann Semple. "Harriet Quimby: America's First Aviator." *Overland Monthly.* December 1911.
6- Oliver Jensen. *The Revolt of American Women.* Harcourt Brace & Co. 1952 p. 137
7- *Some Unconventional Women before 1800: Printers, Booksellers and Collectors.* Papers of the American Biographical Society p.40
8- Harriet Quimby. "A Woman's Exciting Ride in A Racing Motor Car." *Leslie's Weekly,* October 4, 1906.
9- Ibid.
10- Harriet Quimby. "Women Automobile Enthusiasts" *Leslie's Weekly,* January 12, 1911.
11- Ibid.
12- Ibid.
13- Ibid.
14-Editorial. *Leslie's Weekly.* October 5, 1911.
15- *Chronicle of the 20th Century* p.87.
16- Ibid p.108.

Chapter Two
1- Julie Opell Klym. "America's First Flight Academy." *AOPA Pilot.* October, 1979.
2- *Harriet Quimby,* "Exploring the Air Lanes." *Leslie's Weekly,* June 22, 1911.
3- Harriet Quimby. "How A Woman Learns to Fly." *Leslie's Weekly,* May 5, 1911.
4- Harriet Quimby. "Flyers and Flying." *Leslie's Weekly*, June 27, 1912
5- Ibid.
6- Harriet Quimby. "How I Won My Aviator's License." *Leslie's Weekly,* August 24, 1911.
7- Harriet Quimby. "How A Woman Learns To Fly." *Leslie's Weekly.* May 25, 1911

8- Julie Opell Klym. "America's First Flight Academy." *AOPA Pilot.* October 1979.

9- Harriet Quimby biographical files, NAS.

10- Harriet Quimby. "Exploring the Air Lanes" *Leslie's Weekly*, June 22, 1911.

11- New York *Times* August 2, 1911.

12- Ibid.

13- Ibid.

14 -Katherine Brooks-Pazmany. *United States Women in Aviation 1919-1929.* Smithsonian Studies in Air & Space #5; p.32.

15- New York *Times*. Obituary February 5, 1964.

16- Elizabeth H. Gregory. "Women's Records in Aviation." *Good Housekeeping* September 1912.

17- Claudia Oaks. *United States Women in Aviation Through World War I.* Smithsonian Studies In Air and Space #2; p.31.

18 *World Magazine* July 14, 1912.

19 Nancy Zerfoss, "Schoolmarm to School Ms." *Changing Education*, Summer 1974, p.23.

20 *Leslie's Weekly* Editorial October 5, 1911.

21 Harriet Quimby. "How A Woman Learns To Fly." Leslie's Weekly, May 25, 1911.

22- Harriet Quimby. "Aviation As A Feminine Sport. *Good Housekeeping*, September, 1912.

23 Harriet Quimby. "Dangers of Flying; How to Avoid Them," Leslie's Weekly. August 31, 1911.

24 Ibid.

25 *Staten Islander.* September 7, 1911.

26 New York *Times*. September 5, 1911.

27- Ibid. September11, 1911.

28- Ibid.

29- Ibid September 10, 1911.

30- Oakes, Claudia. *United States Women in Aviation Through World War I.* Washington, D.C. Smithsonian Studies in Air and Space #2, 1979. p.29.

31- Air Service Journal, October 11, 1917.

32- New York *Times, May 12, 1912*

Chapter Three

1-Quimby, Harriet "An American Girl's Daring Exploits." *Leslie's Weekly., May 16, 1912. p.567*

2- Ibid.

3- Ibid.

4- Ibid.
5- Ibid.
6- Ibid.
7- Harriet Quimby. "How I Made My First Big Flight Abroad."*FLY Magazine*. June, 1912. p.7.
8- Harriet Quimby. "An American Girl's Daring Exploits." *Leslie's Weekly*. May 16, 1912. p.567
9- Ibid.
10- Harriet Quimby. "How I Made My First Big Flight Abroad."*FLY Magazine*. June, 1912. p.7
11- Ibid.
12- Harriet Quimby. "An American Girl's Daring Exploits." *Leslie's Weekly*. May 16, 1912. p.568
13- Ibid.
14- Ibid.
15- Harriet Quimby. "How I Made My First Big Flight Abroad." *FLY Magazine*. June, 1912. p.9
16- Ibid.
17- Ibid.
18- Ibid p.10.
19- Editorial. New York *Times* April 18, 1912.
20- Weston, George. Beauty and the Bleriot *Aviation Quarterly* Vol. 6 No. 1. 1980.
21- Ibid.
22- Ibid.

Chapter Four
1- Harriet Quimby. "Flyers & Flying." *Leslie's Weekly*, June 27, 1912.
2- Ibid.
3- Ibid.
4- Nancy Zerfoss, "Schoolmarm to School Ms." *Changing Education*, Summer 1974, p.23
5- *Leslie's Weekly*. June 27, 1912 guest editorial.
6- *Good Housekeeping.* September 1912.
7- Harriet Quimby. "An American Girl's Daring Exploit." *Leslie's Weekly* May 16, 1912.
8- Ibid.
9- Ibid.
10- Photo evidence on file with NASM, Smithsonian Institution.
11- New York *Times* July 13, 1912.
12- Betty Peckham. *Women in Aviation.* New York, Thomas Nelson & sons, Inc. 1945.

13- New York *Times*. July 8, 1912.
14- Ibid. June 21, 1912.

Chapter Five
1 - *FLY* Magazine. June 1912.
2 - New York *Times*. July 5, 1912.
3 - *Leslie's Weekly* quoting from the San Francisco *Call Bulletin* August 1, 1912.
4 - *Boston Globe* July 2, 1912.
5 - Ibid.
6 - A. Leo Stevens. "On the Death of Miss Quimby." *Aeronautics* . August 1912. p.67.
7 - Ibid.
8 - Ibid.
9 - Andre Houpert. "When Aviation Becomes Not Only Dangerous, but Foolhardy." New York *Times*. July 7, 1912,
10 - Ibid.
11 - Walter H. Phipps. "The Dangers of the Lifting Tail." *Aircraft* magazine. August 1912.
12 - *Good Housekeeping*. September 1912.
13 - *New York World*. July 14, 1912.
14 - Ibid.
15 - Amelia Earhart. *The Fun of It*. Introduction. New York. Harcourt Brace. 1932.

Photo credits:
Chapter One: Fig. 1-1,1-2,1-3,1-4, Smithsonian Institution.
Chapter Two: Fig. 2-1, 2-3, 2-4, 2-5, 2-7, 2-9, 2-10, Smithsonian Institution.
Chapter Three: 3-1 author's collection, 3-2, 3-3, 3-4, *Leslie's Illustrated Weekly*/author's collection, Fig. 3-5, 3-6, Smithsonian Institution, Fig. 3-7, 3-8, 3-9, 3-10, *Leslie's Illustrated Weekly*/author's collection.
Chapter Four: Fig. 4-1, 4-2, Smithsonian Institution; Fig. 4-3 *Leslie's Illustrated Weekly*/author's collection; Fig. 4-5, 4-7, Smithsonian Institution.
Chapter Five: 5-1, 5-2, Smithsonian Institution; Fig. 5-3, 5-4, US Postal Service.

Index

More Women's Aviation History from Black Hawk Publishing

Ladybirds - The Untold Story of Women Pilots in America. Henry M. Holden with Capt. Lori Griffith. ISBN 1-879630-11-7. 215 pages. 89 photographs, softcover. $19.95.

Ladybirds II - The Continuing Story of American Women in Aviation. Henry M. Holden & Capt. Lori Griffith. ISBN 1-879630-12-5. 352 pages. 114 photographs, hardcover. $23.95.

Her Mentor Was An Albatross - The Autobiography of Pioneer Pilot Harriet Quimby. ISBN 1-879630-05-2. 157 pages. 38 photographs & illustrations, hardcover. $17.95.

On The Wing - Jessie Woods and The Flying Aces Air Circus. Ann Cooper. ISBN 1-879630-17-6. 160 pages. 59 photographs, hardcover. $23.95.

Use the order form on the following page to order any of these books.

Coming from Black Hawk Publishing in 1994!

Women's Encyclopedia of Aviation.

Straight Up - The Whirly-Girls International Women Helicopter Pilots.

Reaching For the Stars - The History of Women in Space.

TO ORDER

Please circle below the books you are ordering, send this order form along with a check or money order, including $3.00 postage and handling for the first book and $1.00 for each additional title. NJ residents must include 6% sales tax. Mail to:

BLACK HAWK PUBLISHING
P.O. BOX 24
MT. FREEDOM, NJ 07970

or call toll free: (800) 451-4529 for VISA/MC.

Ladybirds - The Untold Story of Women Pilots in America.

Ladybirds II - The Continuing Story of American Women in Aviation.

Her Mentor Was An Albatross - The Autobiography of Pioneer Pilot Harriet Quimby.

On The Wing - Jessie Woods and The Flying Aces Air Circus.

I am including a check or money order for: $_____.

Your Name_____

Address_____

City_____State_____ZIP Code_____

Please allow 3-4 weeks for delivery.